FLORIDA
—*in your pocket*—

D0172303

MAIN CONTRIBUTORS: ERIC AND RUTH BAILEY

PHOTOGRAPH CREDITS
James Davis Travel Photography, title page, 5,
17, 20, 22, 24-25, 26, 29, 30, 34, 38 (top), 39,
41, 42, 43, 44, 47, 49, 51, 56, 58, 59, 60, 74, 78,
81, 86, 89, 90, 96, 98, 99, 105, 111, 112, 113,
124; Eric Bailey 8, 12, 15, 16, 61 (top, bottom),
65, 66, 67, 71, 72, 73, 75, 76, 82, 85, 92, 106;
Eye Ubiquitous 19; Eye Ubiquitous/ Jonas Grau
front cover, back cover, 4, 11, 21, 27, 32-33, 36,
50, 54, 55, 63, 77, 87, 94-95, 101, 103, 109, 118,
119; Nature Photographers/E A Janes 9, 10;
Nature Photographers/Paul Sterry 7, 38
(bottom), 52, 53.

Front cover: Fort Lauderdale beach; title page:
Spaceship Earth and Monorail, Epcot Center,
Orlando; back cover: Art Deco building, Miami Beach.

MANUFACTURE FRANÇAISE DES PNEUMATIQUES MICHELIN

Place des Carmes-Déchaux – 63000 Clermont-Ferrand (France)

© Michelin et Cie. Propriétaires-Éditeurs 1998

Dépôt légal Mai 97 – ISBN 2-06-650201-4 – ISSN 1272-1689

No part of this publication may be reproduced in any form

without the prior permission of the publisher.

Printed in Spain 9-98

MICHELIN TYRE PLC
Tourism Department
The Edward Hyde Building
38 Clarendon Road
WATFORD Herts WD1 1SX - UK
☎ (01923) 415000

MICHELIN TRAVEL PUBLICATIONS
Editorial Department
One Parkway South
GREENVILLE, SC 29615
☎ 1-800 423-0485

CONTENTS

Fantasyland and the Real
   Florida *4*
How to Use this Guide *6*

BACKGROUND
Geography *8*
History *13*
The People and Culture
   21

EXPLORING FLORIDA
Must See *26*
Central Florida *28*
The South *37*
The Everglades 48
The Gulf Coast *50*
The Panhandle *62*
The Northeast *69*
The Atlantic Coast *75*

ENJOYING YOUR VISIT
Weather *82*
Calendar of Events *83*
Food and Drink *88*
Shopping *91*
Entertainment and Nightlife
   97
Sports and Activities *102*

A-Z FACTFINDER
The Basics *108*
A-Z Information *110*

Index *127*

FANTASYLAND AND THE REAL FLORIDA

Florida's theme parks have won such enormous world acclaim that the term the 'Real Florida' has evolved to describe the state's natural sights, undeveloped areas and historic parts that are also worth discovering, like the coastlines and the Keys.

Paddle a canoe through wilderness swamp and you're in the real Florida. Watch cowboys roping calves at a rodeo, welcome the shrimp boats returning to their docks or perhaps walk in dawn solitude along the

The Jaws exhibit at Universal Studios forms part of the 'fantasy' aspect of Florida.

Cinderella's Castle is the centerpiece of Fantasyland at Walt Disney World. The huge complex, 20 miles (32km) south of Orlando, is one of the top tourist attractions in the world and takes days to explore.

glistening white beaches of the Panhandle. Explore the rural hiking trails, historic forts, Civil War battlefields and geological formations and you will begin to understand what the Real Florida is all about.

The State has huge areas of wild and unspoiled countryside where you can discover Florida's rich wildlife, from alligators and turtles, to exotic birds, plants and insects. With over 1000 miles (1,600km) of coastline, Florida has beaches for shelling, swimming, watersports, or simply relaxing and enjoying the sunshine. For the more energetic, Florida offers sporting pastimes for spectators and participants alike.

All this, and theme parks, too, are part of a well-rounded vacation in Florida, where the sun shines all year round.

HOW TO USE THIS GUIDE

This guide is divided into four main sections:

Background sets the scene, with an introduction to the geography of the area, from the Flatlands and the Everglades to the sandy beaches and barrier islands. Next comes an overview of Florida's relatively short but nonetheless colorful history, followed by a look at the people and their culture.

Exploring Florida starts with a suggestion of the top ten sights which should be on everyone's vacation checklist – not an easy task when Florida has so much to offer! The area is then divided into six regions: Central Florida, The South, The Gulf Coast, The Panhandle, The Northeast and The Atlantic Coast. Within each of these regions, the guide provides a tour of the main towns, beaches, landmarks, sights and attractions, providing plenty of ideas for excursions and sightseeing for all tastes and interests.

Enjoying Your Visit provides friendly, no-nonsense advice on day-to-day vacation activities which can make the difference between a good stay and a great one – eating out, shopping, sports, entertainment and nightlife – as well as information about local events and the weather.

A-Z Factfinder is an easy-to-use reference section packed with useful information, covering everything you may need to know on your visit, from tipping to renting cars, or from using the telephone to tourist information offices. **A word of warning:** opening hours and telephone numbers are subject to change, so be sure to double-check first.

The extraordinary looking brown pelican is one of Florida's more common birds. It frequents coastal areas and is unusually approachable.

GEOGRAPHY

In the north, Florida shares borders with Georgia and Alabama. To the east lies the Atlantic Ocean, while the state's western shores are washed by the waters of the Gulf of Mexico. In the south, the Florida Keys curve out into the Straits of Florida. Key West, only 90 miles (150km) from Cuba, is the continent's most southerly point.

The state covers a little over 59,988 sq miles (155,368 sq km). It has 1,197 miles (1,926km) of coastline, with 1,100 miles (1,770km) of fine sandy beaches which come in two shades: golden or white. No place in the state is more than 80 miles (130km) from salt water.

Flatlands and the Everglades

Inland, the landscape is punctuated by nearly ten thousand lakes, ranging from 1 acre (0.4ha) to the 448,000 acres (181,440ha) covered by Lake Okeechobee, the second largest freshwater lake in the continental US.

The mouth of the Suwannee River.

A boardwalk through a corkscrew swamp in the Everglades.

There are 166 rivers, including the Suwannee, immortalized by Stephen Foster's 19C ballad *Old Folks at Home*, and the St Johns. North-flowing from Brevard County to Jacksonville, this served as the main highway for Florida's early tourists. The rivers are fed by more than 300 springs, many of them

attractions in their own right, pumping out vast quantities of amazingly clear water.

Florida is a land of contrasts. In the north and central parts are gently rolling hills, pine forests and citrus groves. In the south swampy grasslands abound. The world-famous Everglades, a unique ecosystem, comprises a 7,000-sq-mile (18,130 sq km) 'River of Grass', a slow-moving, shallow body of water flowing through a thick cover of sedges, grasses and rushes from Lake Okeechobee south to the Gulf of Mexico.

Sandy Beaches and Barrier Islands

The Atlantic and Gulf coastlines are both protected by strings of barrier islands, most set just a mile or two offshore. Some are

Flamingo in the southern Everglades is one of many places where you can see the ubiquitous alligator.

Away from the main tourist attractions, Florida has a wealth of fine beaches, such as this one at Key West.

Watching dolphins off Captiva Island, West Florida.

wildlife refuges. Others house well-developed resorts and communities and are connected to the mainland by causeways or bridges. Some measure up to the popular notion of an island paradise, like any in the Pacific. South of Miami, the Florida Keys form a 220-mile (354-km) arc of islands and atolls fringed with mangroves and harboring off their shores the only living coral reef in continental US (*see* p.41).

Islands and beaches naturally go together. The beaches of the southwest Gulf Coast are lovely, but some of the state's best beaches – indeed, some of the best beaches in the country – fringe the Panhandle. Here, on the northwest strip wedged between Alabama and the Gulf, lie those famous squeaking, sugar-white sands of pure quartz.

Northern Florida and the central region north of Orlando are where you will find the state's highlands. But don't worry if you suffer from vertigo. The highest point in Florida – at Lakewood, near the Alabama border – is only 345ft (105m) above sea level.

HISTORY

Archaeologists say tribes of nomadic hunter-gatherers first arrived in Florida some 10,000 years ago, drawn by a warm climate and an abundance of game and fish. Around 5,000 BC semi-permanent settlements began to appear. Like modern Floridians, these people were fond of seafood – the huge mounds of discarded shells they left can be found to this day. They were an enterprising people, hunting and fishing and making tools, utensils and jewelry from the shells. A thousand years before the birth of Christ they began growing crops, and they were making pottery about 800 years before anyone else in the continental US.

Spanish Explorers

Like many of today's visitors, the first Europeans to arrive came in search of a dream. Don Juan Ponce de León, like other Spanish explorers, was mainly looking for gold. He had served with Columbus during his second voyage to the New World, landed near the St Johns River in northeast Florida at the beginning of April 1513 and named the new land after *Pascua Florida*, the Spanish Festival of Flowers. He sailed down to the Florida Keys, then up the west coast. There he met a hostile reception from natives when he attempted to land at Charlotte Harbor, near the present city of Fort Myers. After this episode, de León returned to Puerto Rico.

Eight years later, Ponce de León returned to Charlotte Harbor with two ships, 200 men and 50 horses, determined to establish a settlement and convert the Native Americans to Christianity. The Spaniards were greeted by a cloud of arrows. Ponce de León was among the survivors who retreated to Cuba, where he soon died from his wounds.

In the next 40 years, some 2,000 Spaniards died while trying to colonize Florida and convert the Native Americans.

Spain finally secured a toehold when an expedition led by Pedro Menéndez de Avilés landed on the northeast coast on 28 August, 1565, the Feast of St Augustine. In successfully setting up a colony appropriately named St Augustine, a rivalry was established that continues to this day. Pensacola, in the western Panhandle, claims seniority as the country's oldest established European settlement, while St Augustine claims it is the oldest such settlement continuously occupied.

British Colonists

Already firmly established in other parts of North America by the 18C, Britain began to cast envious eyes at Florida. Privateers raided Spanish galleons and British troops repeatedly attacked St Augustine.

In 1763, under the First Treaty of Paris, the British acquired Florida in exchange for Havana, which had fallen into their hands during the Seven Years War. The British got on reasonably well with the Native Americans, and immigrants from Ireland and other parts of the British Isles soon built up settlements. Florida was content to remain loyal to the Crown when the American Revolution started in 1776.

After Independence

With Britain distracted by the rebellion further north, Spain marched into Pensacola and took control over west Florida. In 1783, the Second Treaty of Paris handed the whole territory back to Spain, but the Spanish had no more luck than they had in the past. There were skirmishes with the Seminole Indians (who had migrated to Florida from other parts of the southeast US) and raids by white settlers from neighboring American states. In 1821, the US wiped out Spain's $5 million debt in exchange for Florida.

A part of Florida's early turbulent history is re-enacted at St Augustine.

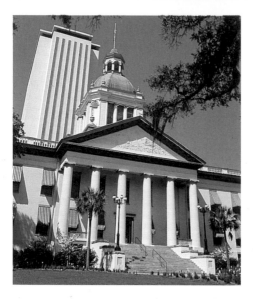

The old and the new Capitol buildings in Tallahassee.

More trouble broke out as land-hungry settlers upset the Seminoles, leading to all-out war in 1817. A raid by General Andrew Jackson in 1817-18 restored a shaky peace, but war broke out again with the Seminoles in 1835 after the US Government began to relocate them to reservations in the West. The Seminole leader, Osceola, whose 4,000 warriors had kept 10,000 American troops busy, was deceitfully arrested while riding under a flag of truce in 1837. After his death a year later, all but 300 of his followers were transported to Oklahoma.

Florida achieved statehood in March 1845, with Tallahassee designated as the capital, a compromise between the twin capitals of Pensacola and St Augustine that had served Florida's two provinces under Spanish rule.

New settlers arrived, attracted by the climate and the prospects of a good living from Florida's expanding trade in sugar, cotton, tobacco, rice and indigo.

At the start of the Civil War in 1861, Florida was committed to slavery and joined the Confederacy. When peace returned in 1865, the state had lost 5,000 lives and sustained $20 million in damage to commerce, industry and homes.

The Rail Barons

Tourism started in northern Florida in the 1850s with steamboat trips along the St Johns River. At that time, much of the state was a swampy wilderness, inaccessible to all but the hardiest of pioneers. Two railroad barons – Henry B Plant and Henry Morrison Flagler –

Today a road, the Overseas Highway, links the Florida Keys, but the first spectacular chain of bridges was built for a railway.

made access easier in the late 19C. They developed lines down each of Florida's coasts and built resort hotels as they went along.

Plant's Atlantic Coast Railroad extended from Richmond, Virginia, to Tampa, where his grand Tampa Bay Hotel, built in Moorish style, remains as a landmark. Flagler pushed his Florida East Coast Railway from Jacksonville south to Palm Beach and on to Miami. He went on to extend the line through the Keys, where it was known as the Overseas Railway as it leapt from island to island on daringly engineered bridges and causeways. Key West was reached in 1912. A hurricane destroyed the Overseas Railway in 1935, but its route and many of its bridges were used to form the Overseas Highway that now connects Homestead, on the edge of the Everglades, with Key West.

During World War II, thousands of service men and women were posted to the Sunshine State. When peace came, many of them returned to settle.

The National Aeronautics and Space Administration (NASA) began operations from Cape Canaveral in 1958. Since then the state has seen the launching of the first earth satellite, the first manned trip to the moon and the development of space shuttles.

Florida found the symbol of youth in the shape of Mickey Mouse, who arrived with the opening of the Magic Kingdom at Walt Disney World on 1 October, 1971. Now Disney World is a major tourist attraction for families from around the world.

The State at Work

Although tourism forms the most conspicuous industry from the visitor's point of view, it is not the only way Florida makes its

money. Even in Metropolitan Orlando, center of the fantasy trade, only one job in five relates to tourism. Orlando itself supports computer and other high-tech industries. Miami boasts an international finance center and an important seaport.

The space shuttle, Columbia, waits for its next mission from the Kennedy Space Center.

All around the coast thriving fishing fleets bring home enormous catches, especially of shrimp and other shellfish. Inland, citrus groves supply the world with oranges, grapefruit and lemons, while Kissimmee (just south of Orlando) and Homestead on the edge of the Everglades are ranching areas.

The modern face of Florida, downtown Miami.

THE PEOPLE AND CULTURE

Orlando sometimes may give the impression that Floridians are amiable extroverts employed in the entertainment industry. If they're not dressed as cartoon characters, you might think they're riding horses, driving speedboats, swimming with killer whales or doubling as film stars. But they are much more diverse than these stereotyped images!

Native Americans

Most of the Natives who lived in Florida when the Spaniards arrived were soon wiped out by disease, slavery, or warfare. The few who survived were taken to Cuba when Spain handed the state to Britain in 1763. The state's longest-standing inhabitants now are the Seminole Indians, originally a branch of the Creek tribe, who migrated to Florida from the southeastern states in the early 17C.

You will find the people of Florida friendly and helpful.

When Florida returned to Spanish control, the Seminoles began making raids into Georgia, and white settlers there complained that the Spaniards were failing to keep the Native Americans in check. Actions by the American army led to the First Seminole War of 1817-18.

The Seminoles found themselves in more trouble when Florida became a US territory and whites started taking their land. The Second Seminole War began in 1835 and continued until 1842.

The Third Seminole War started in 1855 when a party of Seminoles massacred a team of surveyors, then escaped to the Everglades. Although hostilities ceased after three years, the war did not end officially until a treaty was signed in 1934.

The 2,000 or so Seminoles who live in Florida today mostly live on reservations in

The floodlit walls of the Castillo de San Marcos built by the Spanish loom over the harbor in St Augustine.

the Everglades and on the northwest shore of Lake Okeechobee.

The Miccosukee tribe, a Seminole sub-group, has its headquarters in the middle of the Everglades, along the Tamiami Trail (US 41). There is a visitor center with a shop, displays of native crafts and demonstrations of snake-handling and alligator-wrestling.

The Cubans

Despite breaking ties with Spain in the early 1800s, the Spanish connection is still very noticeable. Spanish is now the state's second language, rapidly catching up with English. However, this Spanish influence has come to Florida second-hand, in a sense.

The heritage consists not so much of the Conquistadors themselves, but of many thousands of Latin Americans who have made their home here. The most influential group has been the Cubans, who have been fleeing to Florida since Fidel Castro's rise to power in 1959. So many Cubans have settled in Miami that one part of the city is known as Little Havana. A much older Cuban community is Ybor City, now part of Tampa, which was founded in 1886 when Vincente Martinez Ybor led a movement of cigar manufacturers into the area. Hand-rolled cigars are still crafted in Ybor City, which enjoys a lively Latin ambience.

Black Americans

Before the Civil War, Africans were shipped to Florida in thousands to provide labor for the plantations and citrus groves. A federal census of 1860 recorded nearly 62,000 black slaves in the state's total population of 140,000.

In those days, Florida was an ambivalent place. The north part of the state allied itself with the Deep South where slaves, regarded more or less as livestock, were bought and sold on the open market and kept in often appalling conditions.

South Florida, wilder, sparsely populated, and therefore freer, served as a refuge for runaway slaves from throughout the Southern states. Many fugitive slaves traveled with the Seminoles on their migration from Georgia. (Seminole derives from the Creek Indian word for runaway.) Today, about 13 percent of Florida's population is black.

True-blue Floridians

Florida has always been an important cattle-rearing region, with the first stock brought by Spanish settlers in the 16C. Florida's early settlers were called Crackers, a term thought to derive from the whip-cracking techniques of the state's early cowboys. Originally, the true Cracker was someone whose ancestors were already settled when Florida became a state. Today, the term refers to the architecture dating from pioneer days.

More native Floridians live in the north than in central or southern Florida. Until the development of the railways, settlement was largely restricted to the north.

Nowadays, migrants from the north far outnumber people born in the state. Apart

The modern sculpture Dropped Bowl of Oranges in Slices and Peels, by Claes Oldenburg and Coosie van Bruggen, can be seen in Downtown Miami.

from tourists and 'snowbirds' (escapees from the long winters of Canada and the northern states), newcomers are now arriving in record numbers. The biggest influx in recent years has been from senior citizens – approximately 25 percent of the state's population is more than 60 years old. Low taxation is an added bonus to the appealing climate and the laid-back lifestyle.

MUST SEE

Florida, the Sunshine State, has something for everyone, whether you're looking for the thrill and excitement of the theme parks or the beauty and tranquility of the forests, wetlands and lakes. The range of attractions is almost endless, and which you choose to visit will not only be related to your interests and holiday objectives, but will also depend on the time you have available. Many people return to Florida again and again – there's something new to see and do every time. Listed here are the top ten most popular attractions, grouped by area, starting with Orlando.

Epcot Center, opened in 1982.

One of Orlando's best-known attractions; Sea World.

Top Ten Most Popular Attractions

1. **Walt Disney World★★★**, Lake Buena Vista near Orlando, including the Magic Kingdom, Epcot Center, Disney MGM Studios and Animal Kingdom.
2. **Universal Studios★★★**, Orlando
3. **Sea World★★★**, Orlando
4. **Wet 'n Wild**, Orlando
5. **Kennedy Space Center★★★**, Titusville
6. **Cypress Gardens★**, Winter Haven
7. **The Florida Aquarium★**, Tampa
8. **Busch Gardens★★**, Tampa
9. **Lion Country Safari★★**, West Palm Beach
10. **The Art Deco District★★★**, Miami Beach

CENTRAL FLORIDA

The area around Orlando offers a wide
range of activities, from the famous theme
parks to dramatic forests and beautiful lakes.

Orlando★★★

You can sneer if you like and insist that
you're at **Walt Disney World★★★** purely for
the children's sake, but if you're honest, you
will have to admit that you're impressed.
Everything is on such a grand scale, and so
well organized. Lines move quickly and the
attractions work with 21C magic and pizzazz.
If you're planning to do the whole works,
allow four or five days, but it is still advisable
to arrive early in the day. For best value, get
the multi-day pass. It gives access to all the
different areas of the massive site, which
opened in 1971 to become a top world
vacation spot.

There are four main theme parks on the
Lake Buena Vista site – Magic Kingdom,
Epcot Center, Disney MGM Studios and
Animal Kingdom, which is new for 1998 –
and these sub-divide into many separate
entertainments.

The Walt Disney World entrance is
20 miles (32km) south of Orlando at I-4 and
State Road 192. If you plan to explore the
Epcot Center, or to check in at one of the
themed hotels in the Disney Village Resort
first, use Exit 26B, one exit east.

The Magic Kingdom★★★, the original part
of Walt Disney World, is of special appeal to
small children, who can be photographed
with Mickey and Minnie Mouse, Donald
Duck and other characters. They can visit
Main Street USA, **Fantasyland** (with
Cinderella's Castle), **Tomorrowland**,
Frontierland, **Adventureland**, **Liberty Square**

The entrance to the Chinese Pavilion at Epcot Center.

and **Mickey's Starland**, the attraction that opened to mark the famous mouse's 60th birthday. There are at least 50 rides in the Magic Kingdom, including – for the daring – Space Mountain, Thunder Mountain, and Extra TERRORestrial Alien Encounter.

Epcot Center★★★ (Experimental Prototype Community of Tomorrow) has more cerebral appeal, with pavilions representing different countries and the special effects of the **Spaceship Earth** time machine and **Future World**.

In **Disney MGM Studios★★★**, visitors go behind the scenes of movies and TV shows seeing spectacular stunts and experiencing thrilling rides like the Tower of Terror.

The new **Animal Kingdom★★★** theme park is a mix of thrilling rides, lush landscapes and encounters with real, imaginary and even extinct animals.

To cool off, why not visit one of Disney's three waterparks on the site; have fun in the water or relax on the poolsides.

Like Disney MGM Studios, **Universal Studios Florida** is a working film and TV production complex with movie-themed attractions, rides and stunt shows. Walking around this still-expanding complex, you move from realistic sets of New York or Hollywood, where celebrity look-alikes add

Universal Studios, one of the largest working studios outside Hollywood.

to the make-believe atmosphere of the place.

Adventure rides enable visitors to experience the thrills and spills from films such as *Earthquake, King Kong, Back to the Future, Terminator 2 3D* and *Jaws*. Some of the effects are terrifyingly real. For example, in **Back to the Future – the Ride**, a seven-story Omnimax screen convincingly transports you into an erupting volcano. A new addition is the interactive 'live' **Hercules and Zena Show** where you can fight exotic creatures and Evil Gods. **Twister** is also new – try experiencing life 20 feet from a tornado!

A popular venue, especially for younger visitors, is the **Animal Actors Show**, with a cast of famous animal and bird film stars. Other attractions, such as **Ghostbusters** and a replica of the **Psycho** house, give the audience a chance to take part in the action.

A planned expansion, to be called Universal Florida, will provide five themed hotels, a night-time entertainment complex, shops, an 18-hole PGA golf course and a championship tennis center. The first part of the expansion, with two hotels, is expected to be completed in early 2000.

To see the two new features at **Sea World of Florida★★★**, 'Wild Arctic' and 'Manatees: The Last Generation?', take the Sea World Drive exit off I-4 in Orlando. Among the sea creatures there are killer whales, dolphins, sea turtles and the deadly denizens of the 'Terrors of the Deep' exhibit.

One of Orlando's newest theme parks is **Splendid China**, complete with a scaled-down replica of the Great Wall, terra-cotta warriors and many other well-known Chinese sights.

Given Florida's steamy climate, it's not surprising that water parks are immensely popular – places that make the

neighborhood swimming pool seem dull in comparison. Orlando's **Wet 'n Wild** has 25 acres (10ha) of rides, slides and flumes – all of which finish up in water. One ride equals the height of a seven-story building. There's also a special area for toddlers.

For those who would rather stay dry, **Water Mania** at Kissimmee offers a huge

Cool off at Wet 'n Wild.

maze, arcade games and mini-golf in addition to a spectacular collection of slides. **Gatorland★**, between Kissimmee and Orlando on the Orange Blossom Trail, houses 5,000 alligators and crocodiles in its extensive pools, lakes and creeks. You can watch demonstrations of alligator wrestling and see the creatures jump from the water for a lunch of whole chicken. Alligator meat is presented on the menu at the restaurant!

At Winter Haven, 45 minutes southwest of Orlando is **Cypress Gardens★**, established in the mid 1930s. Plants from 90 countries, a butterfly conservatory, rides and the renowned formation water ski team are among the attractions – to say nothing of the famous Southern Belles gracing the grounds with their elegant gowns and parasols.

As a change from Orlando's theme parks, take a short drive to nearby Winter Park for a visit to the **Charles Hosmer Morse Gallery of Art★**, renowned for its collection of 4,000 objects. Art Nouveau pieces by Louis Comfort Tiffany include paintings, jewelry, lamps and stained-glass windows.

Barely 40 minutes north of Orlando by car, the lakeside village of **Mount Dora** could be

Southern Belles stroll around Cypress Gardens.

on a different continent. With its hilly (but not steep) streets, it could be a place in Britain – in fact, its sister town is Forres in Scotland. Famed for its antiques district, Mount Dora is located in the heart of what Floridians regard as the Central Highlands, a region of lakes and rolling terrain varying from 50-190ft (15-58m) above sea level. The area offers canoeing, boating, fishing, waterskiing, horseback riding, gliding and skydiving.

If you fancy a day out doing next to nothing, you could take the **Rivership Romance** from Sanford, north of Orlando, for a leisurely cruise along the St Johns River.

Less than an hour's drive north of Orlando, downtown **DeLand** is a delightful example of the kind of America that used to feature on the front covers of the *Saturday Evening Post*. Three areas, including Stetson University – named after the Western hat-maker – are designated **National Historic Districts**. Southeast, by 15 miles (24km) is the village of **Cassadaga**, a community of clairvoyants with a center for psychic studies.

Ocala National Forest★ at Alexander Springs is one of Florida's three national forests, situated about 90 minutes north of Orlando's theme parks. You can rent a canoe for a 7-mile (11-km) paddle through swamp and forest, with a truck to retrieve you at the end of the trip.

Ocala★ is the center of Florida's horse-breeding industry. Two-thirds of the state's horse ranches can be found here, as you might guess from the miles of white fencing and the sleek creatures grazing in lush pastures. A different kind of horsepower can be found in Don Garlits **Museum of Drag Racing**. **Silver Springs**, east of Ocala, offers glass-bottom boat rides and jungle cruises.

THE SOUTH

Here the Atlantic meets the Gulf, with the glamour of Miami contrasting with the secluded Everglades and the Florida Keys.

Miami★★★

Forget *Miami Vice* – there's more to Miami than cops and car chases. Look at the wealth of architecture and lush, decorative foliage cascading over rows of balconies. In addition, the climate of greater Miami is sub-tropical, with parks providing welcome shade. Causeways cross Biscayne Bay to link Miami on the mainland with Miami Beach. The futuristic and efficient Metro-mover, a 4.4-mile (7-km) elevated rail line used by commuters, helps keep a considerable amount of road traffic out of the downtown area.

A world finance center, Miami is also an ideal vacation spot, with cruise ships heading out of port for the Caribbean, a number of sights to see around the city and the Everglades just a short 1-hour drive away.

Some of the communities of Greater Miami are visitor attractions in themselves: **Little Havana**, where thousands of Cubans settled after Castro's coup in the early 1960s; fashionable **Coconut Grove★★**, one of Miami's oldest neighborhoods; and **Coral Gables★★**, built by developer George Merrick in the 1920s in the Mediterranean Revival with piazzas and grand entrances. A 90-minute **Old Town Trolley Tour**, with narration, will put you in the city picture. You can hop on and off at various stops along the route.

Animals and sea creatures always seem to hold a special fascination for children, and there's certainly a wide choice of species to be seen in Florida's zoos and aquariums. Miami's **Metrozoo★★** is one of the largest cageless zoos

The famous Art Deco district of Miami Beach.

in America, with 250 species of animals at home in 300 acres (120ha) of simulated habitats. An elevated monorail transports visitors around the park.

Performing dolphins and other marine creatures are popular. In addition to the shows, starring a modern-day Flipper the

The beautiful city of Coral Gables has many architectural treasures, such as this church.

The stunning scarlet ibis can be seen at Metrozoo (left).

dolphin and Lolita, the killer whale, **Miami Seaquarium**★ features a refuge for sea turtles, manatees and sea birds.

Giant insects, marine creatures and reptiles can be seen in the wildlife section at the **Miami Museum of Science and Space Transit Planetarium**. Daily star shows and weekend laser shows are held under the planetarium's 65-ft (20-m) dome.

Set in formal gardens on Biscayne Bay, **Vizcaya Museum**★★★ is an Italian Renaissance-style villa filled with art works and antiques. It was completed in 1916.

Downtown Miami has the **Metro-Dade Cultural Center**★, a Mediterranean-style complex housing the **Miami Art Museum**★, which offers a constantly changing program of international exhibitions as well as a permanent collection.

The **Gusman Center** is one of the major centers for performing arts.

Miami Beach★★★ is famous for its **Art Deco District**★★★, at South Beach, where you can see more than 800 buildings in the famous architectural style of the 1920s through to the 1950s.

Take a trip back to the days of the Renaissance at the Vizcaya Museum.

The **Bass Museum of Art★** in Miami Beach holds an eclectic collection of European art.

Miami Beach offers more than a dozen beaches, with one or two favored by gays, and even the odd patch where a few women go topless. This is illegal unless on a private secluded beach, but some foreign visitors – usually Europeans – risk prosecution.

Eleven miles (18km) south of Miami is **Parrot Jungle** (opened in 1936), where birds take to bicycles and more than 1,100 exotic birds can be admired.

In the same area, north of Homestead, is **Monkey Jungle**, where some of nature's comedians leap about freely, observed by visitors in caged walkways. You can even see monkeys in their swimming pool.

Homestead, the southernmost part of Dade County, has made a good recovery after the pounding it took from Hurricane Andrew in 1992. Cowboys meet here for rodeos and cattle auctions. More than 500 varieties of fruits, nuts and spices from around the world grow at the 20-acre (8-ha) **Fruit and Spice Park**. A local curiosity is **Coral Castle★**, built single-handedly over 30 years by a 100-lb (7-stone) Latvian immigrant after he was jilted by his fiancée in 1923.

The Florida Keys

The Keys stretch 110 miles (177km) from Key Largo next to the mainland to Key West. A road links the line of islands, crossing the turquoise sea on a series of bridges. From Miami it is about three hours by car to Key West. If you don't mind the extra expense, try flying one way and driving the other.

Like much of the US, Florida citizens exhibit a growing 'green awareness'. Voluntary initiatives and new legislation help to prevent overdevelopment and protect the natural environment, such as coral reefs.

Part of the only living coral reef in the continental US is contained in **John Pennekamp Coral Reef State Park★★**, Key Largo, the country's first underwater state park. This vulnerable environment is being

Boats moored at Holiday Harbor in Key Largo.

protected by federal legislation and the cooperation of boaters and divers. Artificial reefs, which provide additional habitats for marine life, are also appearing in the Keys.

Much of this state park is submerged, but the 2,300 acres (930ha) on the mainland contain many rare and endangered plants. Swimming, snorkeling, fishing, picnicking and camping are available. Glass-bottomed boat, canoe and motorboat tours, a snorkeling tour, scuba-diving lessons and sailboat rentals are offered by concessionaires in the park.

Further down the Keys, the **Theater of the Sea** at Mile Marker 84.5 on Windley Key is set in a flooded quarry that once provided ballast stones for Henry Flagler's Overseas Railway. Performances take place throughout the day. Visitors can swim with the dolphins, but reservations are required.

On the island of Vaca Key, about halfway down the Florida Keys, the town of **Marathon** is a diving and snorkeling center that also offers sport fishing charters. The island's airport has daily connections with

Look out for the giant barracuda swimming along the coast of the Keys.

Miami and Key West. The **Museums of Crane Point Hammock** are also on Marathon, which got its name from the frenzied efforts to build Flagler's railway (*see* below) over a 7-mile (11-km) stretch of ocean.

Between Marathon and Key West you will find wildlife refuges for deer and the great white heron, while the waters of the Keys form part of a national marine sanctuary.

The most southerly city in mainland US, **Key West★★★** has known a volatile history –

Tourism has not spoiled the atmosphere of Key West.

The old lighthouse and military museum at Key West.

hammered by hurricanes, haunted by pirates and hit by economic disaster. At one time its residents earned their living as shipwreckers, a respectable, government-regulated activity in early Key West. Rail tycoon Henry Flagler brought prosperity with his Overseas Railway, until it was destroyed by the 1935 hurricane. Since then, the Overseas Highway has revived tourism. This lively yet laid-back little place, best explored via the eccentric **Conch Train**, offers many attractions, including **Ernest Hemingway's House★★**, **Sloppy Joe's Bar** – Hemingway's old haunt – a **Wreckers' Museum**, **Audubon House**, an **Aquarium**, several 19C forts, a notable artist colony and the beautiful, well-preserved architecture of the early 1900s.

The remote **Dry Tortugas National Park★** – including Fort Jefferson, the country's largest 19C coastal stronghold – is located 69 miles (109km) beyond Key West.

Big Cypress National Preserve

Big Cypress begins 30 miles (48km) west of Miami on US 41. Its visitor center is 20 miles (32km) farther along the same road. You would be very lucky to see a Florida panther in the wild, but a diligent search in Big Cypress, north of the western Everglades at Ochopee, could be rewarded with the discovery of panther tracks in wet marl.

Black bears also live in the Big Cypress, which is just about the last bastion of the Florida rockland – a rough limestone soil on which pines and broad-leaved tropical plants grow. Farming and urban development have led to the loss of 98 percent of Florida rockland.

Visiting yachtsmen discovered **Naples★**, on the western edge of Big Cypress, more than a century ago. Today the city calls itself 'Golf Capital of the World' because of the 40 courses on its doorstep, but its appeal extends to anglers, sunbathers, birdwatchers and boaters.

Peace and serenity prevail along the Florida National Trail.

In this area with miles of talc-soft sand, the temperature rarely drops below 60°F (15.5°C) or soars above 90°F (32°C), and rich stocks of fish cry out for bait. For the epicure, jumbo shrimp, snow crabs and scallops go straight from dockside to restaurant.

Quieter souls may be more interested in **Frannie's Teddy Bear Museum**, that displays hundreds of teddies, both old and new.

Just south of Naples you will find **Marco Island**, now tarnished with a rash of high-rise hotels and condominiums.

Florida National Trail

More than 30 miles (48km) of the Florida National Scenic Trail pass through Big Cypress Preserve. Winter, the dry season, is the best time for hiking. Originated by volunteers more than 25 years ago, the trail currently provides some 1000 miles (1,600km) of hiking and will extend 1,300 miles (2,090km) when completed, leading from Big Cypress to the hardwood forests in the state's far northwest corner.

The Florida Trail weaves through numerous wilderness areas. Freely accessible with occasional campgrounds, it provides a chance to observe varied wildlife – raccoon, fox squirrels, river otters, armadillos, bobcat and deer. Bird species include the turkey, snowy egret, osprey, blue heron, purple gallinule and burrowing owl.

In state and national parks throughout Florida there are trails for hiking, biking,

horseback riding and canoeing. Some are in extremely remote areas, where it is wise to be equipped for self-sufficiency. Register with the ranger station or visitor center before attempting any wilderness hiking.

The Everglades

West of Miami, the **Everglades** form a unique and fragile ecosystem, virtually a 'river of grass' some 50 miles (80km) wide and only six inches (15cm) deep. Part of the 1.4 million acreage (566,560ha) of the Everglades is a **National Park★★★**, with visitor centers and board-walks for viewing wildlife.

Much of this vulnerable area could have been lost to development if it had not become a national park in 1947. As it is, the water requirements of agriculture and populated areas of southern Florida mean that in some winters and springs the Everglades is drier than it would naturally be, placing wildlife and vegetation habitats in peril. However, the rainy summer months may help the water level to rise. At one time a canal system was built to drain water from the Everglades. Now restoration projects aim to reverse the damage caused by this drainage.

To the inexperienced eye, the Everglades appear to be a vast region of hardwood hammock (scattered islands of trees), saw grass, stunted cypresses, mangroves and brackish channels. Spend some time becoming familiar with this unique ecosytem. Take a ranger-led nature walk or one of the several narrated cruises that depart from Flamingo.

The National Park has five visitor centers. The main one, at Park Headquarters, is near the park entrance 12 miles (19km) southwest of Homestead on Route 9336.

Exploring the Everglades by boat.

Others are at Royal Palm, Shark Valley, Flamingo and Everglades City. Pick up a map and information leaflets, then enjoy yourself on the boardwalks and trails. Remember that in winter mosquitoes are less active (*see* p. 83).

Guided tours and canoe and houseboat rentals are available from the **Flamingo Visitor Center**, which is at the Everglades' southern tip, at the end of a 38-mile (61-km) road from the main visitor center. Guided tram trips into the Everglades go from Shark Valley, west of Miami on US 41 (the Tamiami Trail), and include viewing from an observation tower.

Off the western side of the Everglades lie the mangrove-laden **Ten Thousand Islands****, formed from seaweed, shell and driftwood trapped in the roots of the mangroves.

49

THE GULF COAST

Discover the interesting shoreline of the Gulf of Mexico, from the shell islands off Fort Myers to Tampa and beyond.

Shelling

Some of the up-market resorts on the Lee Island Coast in southwestern Florida are ideal for a pastime that both local residents and vacationers enjoy – shell collecting. It may begin as a pastime, but it quickly becomes an obsession.

Sanibel Island★★ is one of the world's greatest shelling beaches. The 'Sanibel stoop' is a recognized posture as people search the sand and put their discoveries in a pail. You can't consider yourself a real collector unless you're out there at dawn, at Bowman's Beach or on the hunting grounds of neighboring **Captiva Island★★**, finding what has washed in overnight.

If you want to take life a bit easier, visit Sanibel Island.

Relaxing in the sun on the Gulf Coast.

Sand dollars, horse conchs and all sorts of colorful shells in many shapes may be found. The law discourages the taking of live shells and prohibits the collection of endangered species. Information leaflets are available from local shops and the Tourist Information office.

A local expert, Mike Fuery, operates shell charters. Half-day and full-day shelling tours of some of the offshore barrier islands leave

51

from 'Tween Waters Marina on Captiva Island. Bluenose dolphins are usually seen during the trip.

To see an array of creatures in the wild, go very early in the morning, or just before dusk, to the **J N 'Ding' Darling National Wildlife Refuge★★** on Sanibel Island. You are likely to see alligators, turtles, raccoons, roseate spoonbills, herons and waterfowl. You may also see the graceful, long-necked anhinga. Because its wings are not waterproof like those of many other water

The menacing look of an American alligator.

An anhinga, a typical wetland bird, drying its wings.

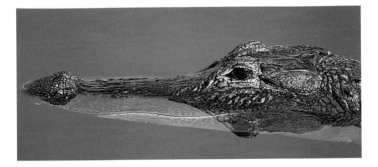

birds, the anhinga must spread its wings to dry in the sun.

In historic **Fort Myers**, inventor Thomas Edison and automotive pioneer Henry Ford had neighboring **winter houses★★** beside the Caloosahatchee River. Both properties are now open to the public. Across the street from **Edison's Home★**, you can visit his laboratory, which contains original equipment. Outside, you can enjoy the shade of one of the world's largest banyan trees. Fort Myers is a noted yachting center and gateway to the idyllic islands of Sanibel and Captiva (*see* above).

In nearby **North Fort Myers**, at the **Shell Factory**, you'll see a lot of beautiful shells. A free guided tour of the shell processing facility and the corals and shells made into jewelry and ornaments is available at what claims to be the largest display of shells and coral in the world.

Sarasota★★, about an hour's drive south of Tampa, is a pleasant, quiet holiday spot, ideal for relaxation. Sun-worshippers have a good choice of beaches along the Gulf barrier islands with places such as Anna Maria Island, Bradenton Beach, Siesta Key and

Longboat Key. The latter Key is famed for its **Avenue of Flowers**, a quaint arcade of art and craft boutiques and sidewalk restaurants. Sarasota's major cultural attractions are

Help in an emergency is never far away on the beaches of Florida.

Cà d'Zan★★, an ornate Venetian-style mansion, the **Ringling Museum of Art★★**, where several Rubens cartoons are displayed, and the **Museum of the Circus**, all built by the circus magnate, John Ringling. Nearby, you will find the **Historic Asolo Theater**, an architectural jewel. The **Asolo Center for the Performing Arts** and the **Van Wezel Performing Arts Hall** are also in Sarasota.

Tampa Bay Area

With an average annual temperature of 73°F (23°C), and an average annual sea temperature even higher at 75°F (24°C), St Petersburg, facing Tampa Bay, and its neighbors on the Gulf of Mexico, form one of Florida's most popular holiday regions. St Petersburg, Clearwater, Tampa and the smaller coastal communities in between lie within a 28-mile (45-km) chain of islands with world-class beaches.

There is plenty of beach for everyone at St Petersburg.

The city of **St Petersburg★★** boasts a thriving arts community, a revamped downtown waterfront and the impressive **Florida Suncoast Dome** that stages sports events and concerts. St. Petersburg's 440-yd (400-m) **Pier★** is a five-story inverted

The Colonial Gardens Hotel in St Petersburg.

pyramid structure containing shops, an aquarium and restaurants.

Not far from the middle of the city, the **Boyd Hill Nature Park** provides 3 miles (5km) of trails and boardwalks They pass through a hardwood hammock, sand pine scrub, willow marsh and lake shore and can be followed on foot or bicycle.

Florida offers a wide range of museums to suit all interests. In St Petersburg, the **Salvador Dalí Museum★★★** houses the world's largest, most comprehensive collection of works by the Spanish surrealist. The **Museum of Fine Arts★★**, near The Pier, is known for its collections of works by the Impressionists and European paintings and sculpture from the 17C and 18C. **Great Explorations★** gives loads of hands-on experiences, including a weird, totally dark Touch Tunnel.

Tampa★★ ranks as Florida's third largest city, with a population of 280,000. It is a thriving business and commercial center occupying a commanding position on Tampa Bay. Tourists have been attracted to the city since 1891, when Henry Plant built the **Tampa Bay Hotel★★** at the end of his Atlantic Coast Railroad line. The hotel, with its distinctive minarets and Moorish architecture, now belongs to the University of Tampa. A section of the hotel has been preserved as the **Henry B. Plant Museum★**. The accent is on amusement as well as education in the **Museum of Science and Industry★★**, the largest of its kind in Florida. The city's busy port is the embarkation point for passengers taking luxury cruises to the Caribbean and on day trips on casino ships.

To get around Tampa and to cross Tampa Bay to St Petersburg, use I-275. You must also experience the beautiful sweeping Sunshine Skyway which spans the 11-mile (18-km) mouth of Tampa Bay. The suspension bridge, its yellow cables illuminated at night, soars 183ft (56m) above the water.

In Tampa, the streets and public buildings are graced with impressive sculptures. The **Tampa Museum of Art** displays a fine collection of Greek and Italian antiquities and expressionist prints, and the **Museum of African-American Art** is the only one of its kind in Florida. The city also boasts **Tampa Bay's Performing Arts Center**.

At Tampa's **Busch Gardens★★: The Dark Continent**, the theme is Africa, as you might guess. Among the 500 species roaming in comparative freedom are hippos, giraffes, gazelles, lions and zebras. There are also spectacular stage shows, white-knuckle rides, bird gardens and a children's play area, Land of the Dragons.

The most northerly of a chain of barrier islands linked to the Pinellas Peninsula by

bridges and causeways, **Clearwater Beach** is a popular holiday destination with excellent beaches and a wide range of accommodations.

Tarpon Springs★, north of Clearwater and Dunedin, supports a Greek community where sponge diving is a major industry. Visit the **Spongeorama Exhibit Center**, or go up the street to the main sponge dock to take the 30-minute cruise to see a sponge-diving demonstration.

With three national forests totalling more than 1 million acres (404,700ha), 15 national parks and more than 100 state parks, Florida can provide miles of countryside in which to wander, watch wildlife or picnic. Primitive camping is permitted in some of the state parks, and others offer full camping facilities.

Florida's native wildlife, such as the black bear, the Florida panther (an endangered species), the alligator and the venomous

The Python Ride at Busch Gardens, (above left).

Take the steam train to get a close-up view of the animals at Busch Gardens.

There are many boat tours that you can take from Clearwater Beach.

snakes (of which Florida has six species, the most deadly being the coral snake), should all be treated with respect. All of them prefer to avoid confrontation, except for the poisonous water moccasin snake, which will hold its ground. Whitetail deer are shy and are seldom – if ever – threatening to humans.

A friendlier species is the huge and harmless herbivore, the manatee, which has no natural enemies except humans. The manatee is at most serious risk of injury from boat propellers and fishing lines as it swims hidden beneath the surface. About 90 minutes north of Clearwater, one of the places where injured or orphaned manatees are tended is **Homosassa Springs State Park**. Here you can watch these gentle mammals from an underwater observatory. You can also see many wild animals, birds and reptiles indigenous to the state.

Traveling further north up the Gulf Coast, visit **Cedar Key** for a genuine piece of 'real'

An abundance of wildlife at Homosassa Springs State Park.

Florida . This picturesque little town of sun-bleached timber buildings clinging to the edge of the Gulf of Mexico appeals to artists and vacationers who appreciate the simple life. Most residents earn their living from the sea, and pelicans vie with anglers for the fish they catch from the pier. Boat trips and rentals are available for exploring neighboring islands. The town has a good selection of restaurants and B & B inns, mostly within a short walk of the pier on historic **Dock Street**.

The tranquil setting of Cedar Key.

THE PANHANDLE

This coastline of beaches of the finest white
sand sweeps round from Pensacola to Cedar
Key. All along the Panhandle the sand is
almost pure quartz, washed down from the
Appalachian Mountains over thousands of
years. It squeaks when you walk on it.

Pensacola★, Florida's western-most city, is
a lovely city of bridges and beaches near the
Alabama state line. Here the first European
settlement in the US was established, though
St Augustine claims the title of the country's
oldest permanent settlement. Pensacola has
three extensive historic districts. Historic
Pensacola Village offers streets of restored
homes and commercial buildings that reflect
the lifestyle of 19C northern Florida. The
village includes museums of commerce and
industry and guided tours of half a dozen
historic homes. Among the city's attractions
are the **Pensacola Historical Museum**, the
Civil War Soldiers Museum and the **Museum
of Art**, housed in the old jailhouse. The **Wall
South and Veterans' Memorial Park** is a three-
quarters scale replica of the Vietnam Veterans'
Memorial in Washington, DC. At the impressive (and free) **National Museum of Naval
Aviation★★**, you can see more than 100 aircraft.

Southeast of the city are the **Gulf Breeze
Zoo and Botanical Gardens**, while to the
southwest lies **Fort Pickens★**, where Apache
chief Geronimo was imprisoned. A small fee
buys a seven-day vehicle permit to explore
the **Gulf Islands National Seashore**, a string
of barrier islands in the Gulf of Mexico. This
enormous region of heavenly beaches and
coastal marshes can be accessed from State
Road 292 southwest of Pensacola, and
extends southeast on Santa Rosa Island. It
stretches nearly 150 miles (240km) into the

Every type of watersport is available in Florida.

state of Mississippi. The 18-mile (29-km) stretch of **Santa Rosa Island** is ideal for a day trip from Pensacola.

Perdido Key and **Big Lagoon** provide more than 16 miles (26km) of shoreline. Perdido Key lies 15 miles (24km) west of Pensacola. Perdido Key and Big Lagoon may seem remote, and in pleasantly warm winter weather you may encounter few other visitors, but they are very popular the rest of the year, attracting 5.5 million people annually.

A string of beach communities extend along the Emerald Coast – named for its clear green sea and sugar-white sand – between Pensacola to the west and Panama City Beach to the east. Along this coastline there are more opportunities for recreation than sightseeing – golf, fishing, watersports and birdwatching.

In winter, the temperature in northern Florida will drop below 65°F (18°C) – too cold for the locals, but visitors from colder climates have acres of sand to themselves. Pensacola's major feature is a 40-mile (64-km) stretch of white sandy beaches. **Pensacola Beach**, the main resort area, is reached from the city by a 3-mile (5-km) bridge across Pensacola Bay.

The marine life featured in the **Gulfarium** at **Fort Walton Beach**, along the Panhandle east of Pensacola, offers a supporting cast of performing scuba divers, together with otters and birds. Northeast of Fort Walton Beach, admission is free to the **US Air Force Armament Museum** located at the vast Eglin Air Force Base. Bombs, aircraft and missiles from World War I to the Gulf War are displayed.

Further along the Emerald Coast is a small community that has received international acclaim for its urban plan and architectural design. Developed in the 1980s, **Seaside** captures the ambience of the 19C with its brick-paved streets and white picket fences. Some of the pastel wood-framed cottages, with wide porches and overhanging roofs, are available for weekly rental.

Miniature golf, amusement park rides, video arcades and water parks make **Panama City Beach★** the most popular family vacation destination in the Panhandle – and the beaches are superb. The main areas of activity during the summer months are the **Miracle Strip Amusement Park** and **Shipwreck Island Water Park**, where you can float down the Lazy River on an inner tube or try out more exhilarating rides, including the 35mph (56.3kph) Speed Slide. **Gulf World** provides a close-up view of dolphins, sharks, sea lions and stingrays. Diving history from

Gulls resting on the glorious sands of Panama City Beach.

the 16C to the present can be seen at the **Museum of Man in the Sea**, open all year. Gold and silver treasure from sunken ships is also exhibited. Another of the state's most popular parks, **St Andrew's State Recreation Area** provides a peaceful alternative to the city's amusement parks. Nature trails lead through pine forest, marshes, dunes and around lakes, offering the possibility of seeing deer, raccoons, alligators, waterfowl and shorebirds – and there is safe swimming for children. Fishing piers, boat rentals and full camping facilities are available.

Shell Island, another popular shell-collecting spot with a 7-mile (11-km) shoreline near Panama City Beach, is accessible only by ferry from St Andrew's State Recreation Area, or through one of the private boat companies that offer cruises to the island. During the voyage, you may see dolphins leaping out of the water. However avid a sheller you become, remember that if you return home by air your collection will add considerably to the weight you have to carry. Be selective.

Just outside the small Panhandle town of **Marianna**, northeast of Panama City, you will find **Florida Caverns State Park**. Several times daily there are guided tours of the fascinating network of caves with strangely-shaped calcite formations of stalagmites and stalactites, columns and draperies. The caves that can be visited were discovered in the early 1900s during a hurricane. The rest of this large cave system is closed to the public. Boating, canoeing, camping, swimming, and horseback riding are available in the park.

Greatly under-visited by tourists, possibly because of its geographical position, is **Tallahassee★**, the state capital. A pleasant

The Union Bank in Tallahassee.

city, its canopy roads – green tunnels of giant live oaks festooned with Spanish moss – wind through the countryside. In spring the city is bright with azaleas, huge magnolias and many other blossoms. Boasting more than 120 sites listed on the National Register of Historic Places, the city presents antebellum homes and two state capitols which stand side by side: **Old Capitol★**, a museum, and **New Capitol**, a working government building, but both are open to the public. Visitors may like to experience the concerts given by the city's symphony orchestra. The **Old Town Trolley Tour** provides a useful introduction to the city, which contains two interesting historic districts: **Calhoun Street** and **Park Avenue★**. Tallahassee is home to two universities – Florida State University

See Florida's natural beauty at the Tallahassee Museum of History and Natural Science.

and Florida Agricultural and Mechanical University. **Maclay State Gardens★**, with more than 200 plant varieties, are open year round. The **Tallahassee Museum of History and Natural Science★** provides a 19C farm and native Florida wildlife, including the Florida panther, in extensive natural habitats. A 9-ft (2.7-m) mastodon skeleton discovered in Wakulla Springs is exhibited at the **Museum of Florida History★★**.

East of **Woodville**, about 13 miles (21km) south of Tallahassee, is **Natural Bridge Battlefield State Historic Site★★**, where a battle towards the end of the Civil War saved Tallahassee from attack by Union forces. The battle is re-enacted each March.

One of Florida's most fascinating state parks, offering guaranteed wildlife viewing, is **Wakulla Springs★★**, 16 miles (26km) south of the state capital, Tallahassee. From glass-bottomed boats cruising over one of the world's largest and deepest freshwater springs you can see aquatic life far below in astonishingly clear water. Just as thrilling is a boat trip along the Wakulla River, where knowledgeable guides point out alligators, turtles, snakes, jumping mullet, whitetail deer, raccoons and a medley of waterfowl, including wood ducks and anhingas.

Tallahassee Airport is at the edge of the **Apalachicola National Fores**t – one of Florida's three national forests – which occupies parts of four counties and harbors wild pigs. South of the forest, the coastal road westward along the Panhandle takes you through quaint little towns like **Apalachicola★**, known for its oysters, and **Carabelle**, known for its shrimping fleet and its police station – the world's smallest. It's a telephone booth!

THE NORTHEAST

Settled in early times by the Spanish, English and French, this historic area offers a rich heritage along a verdant coastline protected by barrier islands.

The wide St John's River bisects downtown **Jacksonville★**, a commercial and industrial center covering 850sq miles (2,200sq km) which forms the largest city in area in the US. The city center itself is about 12 miles (19km) inland.

The city is often referred to as **Jacksonville and the Beaches** after the vacation spots of Atlantic Beach, Neptune Beach and Jacksonville Beach that form part of Jacksonville. **Riverwalk** runs along the south bank of the St John's – including more than a mile (1.5km) of sidewalk. **Jacksonville Landing★**, two floors of shops, restaurants, and cafés with musical and street entertainment, sits on the north bank.

An elevated walkway and miniature train provide easy viewing for an African Veldt exhibit at Jacksonville's **Zoological Gardens**. There is plenty to do and see at the **Museum of Science and History★**, with three floors of exhibits, a large marine aquarium and a planetarium. The **Anheuser-Busch Brewery** tour is popular with visitors, who can view the whole brewing and bottling process and sample the product. Noted for its outstanding collection of paintings and sculptures, the **Cummer Gallery of Art and Gardens★★** covers a span from 2000 BC to the present.

Kingsley Plantation★, within the Timucuan Ecological and Historic Preserve, is where cotton and other crops were grown in the 18C and 19C. The story of the original owner, who married a free black woman, is told in pictures and documents.

A five-minute car-ferry ride takes you across St Johns River from Mayport to Fort George Island, where, if you follow the A1A north, you reach **Amelia Island★★**, a blissful region of uncrowded sandy beaches, soaring pelicans, lush greenery, resort hotels, historic bed and breakfast inns and **Fernandina Beach★**, a little town of specialty shops, seafood restaurants, and shrimp boats. Shrimp caught by the local fleet appear on menus of the town's many restaurants. With its brick-paved **Centre Street★** (the spelling recalls a period of British rule), the neat little town of Fernandina Beach lies at the head of Amelia Island, most northerly of Florida's Atlantic coast barrier islands. More than 50 separate Victorian buildings, including the Palace Saloon – the oldest licensed bar in Florida – are on the National Register of Historic Places.

The Atlantic Ocean provides sport for surfers along much of the coast. The extensive beaches of Amelia Island have dunes 40ft (12m) high in places. Sea oats sway gracefully in the breeze, preventing erosion, and notices warn people not to pick them. At dawn all year round, people go out on to the beach to jog, collect shells, to watch shorebirds feeding, or to photograph the sunrise.

There are nearly 20 state camping parks and recreation areas on the coast. **Amelia Island State Recreation Area** is one of the few beaches you can enjoy on horseback. Guided rides are available from Seahorse Stables at Fernandina Beach.

Fort Clinch State Park★★, near Fernandina Beach on Amelia Island, gives a fascinating glimpse of military life during the Civil War. The brick fort is in a good state of repair and uniformed park rangers convincingly play the roles of soldiers in a Union garrison.

Home to the University of Florida, the lively city of **Gainesville**, southwest of Jacksonville, provides sidewalk cafés along its brick-paved Main Street. The **Florida Museum of Natural History★**, which displays prehistoric animal skeletons, is located on the university campus, together with the **Harn Museum of Art★**. **Morningside Nature Center** is a 278-acre (112.5ha) living history farm. The **Devil's Millhopper State Geological Site★**, a 120-ft (36.5-m) deep sink-hole, features rare plants and a number of waterfalls among its lush vegetation.

Nearly five centuries of history live and breathe in **St Augustine★★★**. This was the

The five flags displayed outside this house in St Augustine reflect the town's checkered history.

first permanent European settlement in the
US. To explore this captivating little city,
climb on board one of the bright little open-
sided trains that are provided to give visitors
narrated tours through the streets. You can
get off whenever something takes your fancy,
and re-join your train (or another) when
you are ready. Alternatively, tour the historic
district by stylish horse and carriage.

The massive fortress of **Castillo de San
Marcos★★★**, a national monument, overlooks
Matanzas Bay on the northern Atlantic
coast. Built by the Spanish of coquina (local
stone created by sedimentation of seashells)

*St Augustine has a
vibrant European
flavor.*

There is no hustle and bustle in the Colonial Historic District of St Augustine.

with walls 16ft (5m) wide in places, the fortress, never conquered, remains largely intact. It was completed in 1695, having taken 24 years to construct.

In St Augustine's **Spanish Quarter★**, costumed craftspeople and soldiers chat about the daily lives of 18C citizens. In the streets of the **Colonial Historic District** (which are mostly closed to auto traffic), there are specialty shops, restaurants and street performers. Here you will find the **Oldest Wooden Schoolhouse**, built of cypress and red cedar before 1763. The **Oldest Store Museum**, in Artillery Lane, is packed with goods from the turn of the century – red flannel underwear, the earliest bicycles, toys and a range of household goods. The **Oldest House★★**, which includes a museum, was built immediately after British forces destroyed St Augustine in 1702. Other places of interest include **Flagler College★★**, built in the Spanish Renaissance style in 1888 and **Lightner Museum★★**, which includes superb examples of Tiffany glass and mechanical musical instruments.

The **Government House★★** reflects the city's history, from early native settlement to the 19C, when the railway magnate Henry Flagler made an impact with his grand style of hotel architecture.

Mission de Nombre de Dios★, off San Marco Avenue, marks the site where Pedro Menéndez de Avilés is believed to have landed in 1565.

Florida's original **St Augustine Alligator Farm★★** is on State Road A1A south of St Augustine. Residents include newly hatched alligators and a 1,700lb (770kg) New Guinea crocodile.

Just south of Cape Canaveral is popular Cocoa Beach.

THE ATLANTIC COAST

Beaches

A laid-back lifestyle exists along Florida's Atlantic coast with its world-famous beaches.

There are also quiet beaches where you can get away from it all (below right).

While some of the 1000 miles (1,600km) of Florida's beaches have safe bathing for small children, parents should be aware that many have strong currents (*see* Titusville below). Most of the time tidal movement is minimal, waves lap unaggressively and the beaches slope gently into the water. Be aware too that you may encounter hazards like jellyfish and other stinging creatures. Lifeguards patrol some of the beaches, which are kept in pristine condition. Many beaches are equipped with cold water taps at access points for de-sanding your feet. Further south, palm trees dot some of the beaches and thatched shelters provide shade.

During early summer, with July and August the peak months, sea turtles – loggerheads, leatherbacks and Atlantic green turtles – use Florida's Atlantic coast, between Titusville and Juno Beach, to come ashore at night and lay their eggs in the

sand. The infant turtles risk being swallowed by predators as they make their short but hazardous journey into the sea. Both turtles and eggs are protected by law.

Daytona Beach, the 'Birthplace of Speed', is where early car races took place along the firm sands and where Sir Malcolm Campbell drove at a record 276mph (444kph) in 1935. In 1959 the Daytona International Speedway opened. Today it is still a mecca for car and motorcycle racing enthusiasts – for a small charge you can drive a car along an 18 mile (29km) stretch. For those who enjoy surfing, deep-sea fishing and the pleasures of a popular resort, the Daytona Beach area is very appealing. Its pier features a gondola skyride, a bandshell and a Space Needle ride that provides great views.

Watersport facilities are excellent along the beaches of Marco Island.

The wide expanses of Daytona Beach.

Florida has 15 national parks, including preserves, seashores, monuments and memorials. Of these, six offer recreational activities on the Atlantic coast. Many beaches in the more highly populated areas are high-activity spots during the lazy summer holiday and on weekends. Volleyball is just one of the beach sports played at places like Daytona Beach, Miami Beach and **Fort Lauderdale★**.

Space Coast

To explore the **Space Coast**, drive south of Daytona to the Titusville area. **The John F. Kennedy Space Center★★★** is contained within the Merritt Island National Wildlife Refuge, south of the Canaveral National Seashore that covers more than 80,000 acres (32,375ha).

Spaceport USA is the Space Center's visitor center. After digging deeply in your pocket in the theme parks of Orlando (*see* p.28), you'll

The Rocket Garden at Kennedy Space Center.

welcome the fact that all the space exhibits and the parking are free. However, you will have to purchase tickets to take tours or to see films. There is a nominal charge for the two-hour bus tour of the Space Center or Cape Canaveral Air Force Station. An exciting IMAX film on Spaceport US's activities and *Blue Planet* (a film about earth) are shown on screens five stories high. A full exploration of the Space Center takes about six hours.

There are launch-viewing areas on roads and coastal locations around **Titusville**. Dates of proposed launches are displayed at entrances to the Space Center, or you can call a shuttle hotline for information (☎ 1-800-432-2153). Certain approach roads are closed to public traffic at these times.

The **Astronaut Hall of Fame★**, opened in 1990, is 10 miles (16km) from Kennedy Space Center in Titusville. The site honors the first 20 US astronauts, displaying historic space suits and photography, and showing films.

Canaveral National Seashore, at Titusville, is subject to strong currents and swimming can be dangerous, as is true for other parts of the Atlantic coast. One of the best beach areas, **Playalinda Beach★★**, closes before and during space shuttle launches from the nearby John F Kennedy Space Center. Back-country camping is permitted on the National Seashore's **North Beach** and on the islands at the north end of **Mosquito Lagoon**, except at shuttle launch times. Mosquito Lagoon lives up to its name – take a strong insect repellent.

Several outdoor activities can be enjoyed at **Canaveral**, but birdwatchers are usually the first to arrive. More than 280 bird species have been recorded there. The **Merritt Island National Wildlife Refuge★★** offers slide presentations.

Other Attractions

Located on the appropriately named Gold Coast, **Palm Beach County★★★** is the winter home of the rich and famous. It extends from Jupiter in the north to Boca Raton in the south and includes the upscale communities of Palm Beach and West Palm Beach. The residents in Palm Beach are sensitive to tourists rubber-necking in their exclusive neighborhoods, but visitors can get a back-yard view of some of the grand houses by taking a sightseeing cruise aboard the *Star of Palm Beach* paddle-wheeler along the intracoastal waterway. One mansion which is open to the public is the **Henry M. Flagler Museum★★**, former home of the railroad baron, in Palm Beach. Its lavishly furnished rooms house an extensive collection of antiques, paintings, Oriental rugs and china. Flagler's private railway car is displayed in the grounds.

The headquarters of the Professional Golfers' Association of America and the US Croquet Association are both in Palm Beach County. A popular spectator sport is polo.

The **Norton Museum of Art★★** in West Palm Beach shows works by Chagall, Dufy, Matisse, Monet, Picasso, Pissarro and Renoir.

Lion Country Safari★★, 15 miles (24 km) west of West Palm Beach, was the first drive-through cageless zoo in the US. African animals roam freely through the park's 500 acres (202ha).

Take a sightseeing cruise of the 'Venice of America' – Fort Lauderdale – aboard the **Jungle Queen**, and maybe stop off at an island for a delicious shrimp dinner.

Atlantis, the Water Kingdom, at Hollywood south of Fort Lauderdale, offers a white-water rapids ride, lots of slides and an Olympic-size swimming pool.

Old Port Cove on North Palm Beach.

Rural life is close at hand even in the cities. At **Davie**, a cattle town a few miles west of downtown Fort Lauderdale, the local McDonald's has hitching posts where cowboys can tether their mounts. At **Flamingo Gardens and Arboretum**, also in Davie, take a 1.5-mile- (2.5-km-) long guided tram tour through citrus groves, a rainforest and natural hammock, seeing flamingos, otters and alligators along the way.

WEATHER

Florida has every reason to call itself 'the Sunshine State'. Lying just 100 miles (160km) north of the Tropic of Cancer, the state enjoys a sub-tropical climate with average summer temperatures ranging from 80°F (27°C) in the north to 83°F (28°C) in the south. Winter averages range from 53–68°F (12–20°C). St Petersburg, on the Gulf of Mexico in Central Florida, still basks in the glory of appearing in the *Guinness Book of World Records* for notching up 768 consecutive days of sunshine between 9 February, 1967 and 17 March, 1969.

Rainfall throughout the state averages 53in (135cm) a year – and when it rains it pours. Summer rainstorms can be so violent they might have been created by Walt Disney's animators. Lightning can be deadly, especially on an open beach or golf course. The hurricane season is from June to October. Weather patterns are closely watched by the US National Hurricane Center (in Coral Gables) and local authorities have well-practiced safety and evacuation programs.

It does rain in Florida!

Florida's sub-tropical climate will be a joy to visitors from places where the weather is more volatile, but it calls nonetheless for a little common-sense caution.

The biggest hazard is the danger of sunburn. Some people seem to forget that large areas of their bodies are still exposed to the sun's dangerous rays as they walk around sightseeing. Sunburn doesn't happen only when you're lying on a beach. Wear a hat or cap when you go outdoors, and use a strong sunscreen.

Dress comfortably – shorts and a tee shirt will be fine – and wear good walking shoes on those sightseeing expeditions. Trudging around a theme park in the heat of day can be very hard on the feet.

Make sure your first-aid kit includes an insect repellent. In the summer, parts of Florida, especially near densely wooded and still-water areas, are plagued by its most ubiquitous pest, mosquitoes, as well as tiny sandflies known as 'No-see-ums'.

CALENDAR OF EVENTS

Florida's ethnic and cultural mosaic – to say nothing of its dedication to the fun side of life – ensures a full calendar of festivals and celebrations. Here are some highlights.

January
Tarpon Springs Festival of Epiphany

Florida's Greek community celebrates one of the most important religious festival in the Orthodox calendar, the baptism of Christ in the River Jordan. Pageant begins at the cathedral and participants then parade around Spring Bayou. Here, youths dive into the bayou to recover a wooden cross tossed into the water by the Archbishop.

February
Labelle Swamp Cabbage Festival Located on the northwestern edge of the Everglades, Labelle pays tribute to Florida's state tree, the cabbage, or sabal, palm, whose edible heart was a favorite pioneer food. Country music accompanies the feast.
Tampa, **Gasparilla Pirate Festival** A 'pirate' ship sails into Tampa Bay and 700 swash-buckling sea-dogs take over the city for a day.
Ybor City Fiesta Day Enjoy Latin music and dancing, and free bean soup with Cuban bread and coffee at this colorful fiesta.

March
Arcadia, **All-Florida Championship Rodeo** Calf-roping, saddle bronco riding, bareback riding and bull riding are featured in Florida's oldest rodeo.
Daytona Beach Motorcycle Week Bikers from all over the US roar into town. Lots of Harley-Davidsons are on show.

April
Tallahassee Springtime Festival The state capital celebrates its founding with a big parade.
DeLand Cracker Day The pioneer spirit is revived at a public barbecue with a horse show and traditional crafts.

May
Fernandina Beach Shrimp Festival The fleet is decorated, bands play, and local restaurateurs set up stalls and vie with each other to present shrimp in many guises.
White Springs, **Florida Folk Festival** Music, dancing, crafts and tale-telling at the Stephen Foster State Cultural Center.

The Stephen Foster State Cultural Center, in White Springs.

June
St Augustine, Spanish Night Watch A costumed torchlight procession is led by fife and drum through the Old Spanish Quarter.
Monticello, Jefferson County Watermelon Festival Who can eat the most watermelon? And who can spit the seeds the farthest?

July
Key West, Hemingway Days Or should it be daze? A week of story-telling, sailing, fishing and arm-wrestling is climaxed by the Hemingway Look-alike Contest.

The Ernest Hemingway House in Key West.

August

Palm Beach County Royal Palm Festival The whole county celebrates the stately palm that lines its roadsides with a program of parades, cultural events, sporting contests, song and dance and a seafood feast.

September

Caryville International Worm Fiddling Contest This small community near Bonifay in northwest Florida stages a contest to see who can charm the most worms to the surface. The worms lose – they're used for bait.

Pensacola Seafood Festival Seafood booths

are set up in the streets and there are cooking contests and lots of activities both ashore and on the water.

October
Key West Fantasy Fest To celebrate the day when Key West declared itself a Conch Republic and seceded from the Union, the Conch Republic goes crazy again – this time in a massive Mardi-Gras-style parade with people in fantastic fancy dress.

November
Jacksonville Jazz Festival One of the largest free jazz festivals in the world, with bands playing in parks, squares and by the river.
Greater Fort Lauderdale Film Festival The East Coast's largest film festival showcases more than 100 international films, world premieres and star-studded parties.
Pensacola, **Great Gulfcoast Arts Festival** Artists and contemporary and traditional craftspeople from throughout the US compete for cash prizes in a massive exhibition staged in the city's historic Seville Square.

A giant guitar atop the Hard Rock Cafe, Bayside Marketplace, Miami.

December
Walt Disney World Candlelight Processional takes place annually at Epcot.
Mickey's Very Merry Christmas Party is held in the Magic Kingdom.
Miami, **Miccosukee Arts Festival** Artists and performers of 30 Native American tribes from across the US show off their talents.

FOOD AND DRINK

For anyone who does not like seafood or is allergic to shellfish, there are plenty of alternatives. Almost every restaurant and diner has ribs, steaks, chicken and burgers on its menu. But to ignore the seafood is a bit like boycotting pasta in Italy or sushi in Japan. You can buy oysters by the bucketful for a few dollars at roadside shacks. They are widely available in restaurants, and surprisingly inexpensive. Clams, stone crabs, softshell crabs, crab claws, scallops and shrimp – massive ones that cover the plate – are delectable. Succulent grouper or snapper is served plain or blackened – rubbed with firey spices and pan-seared.

Dining is usually early – turn up after 9pm and you may be unlucky outside major cities. Visitors from other continents will probably find the portions too large. Most restaurants are happy to split a dish – for a small extra charge you can order a single entrée for two people to share.

Make a brief lunchtime stop for a sandwich and you could find yourself munching a thick hamburger layered with lettuce, tomato, and served with fries.

In the laid-back Florida Keys, as in bars all over the US, happy hour is a nightly ritual. People enjoy a drink and watch the sunset.

All the major cities have a variety of ethnic restaurants. Cuban and Nicaraguan, as well as Italian, Chinese, Greek, Mexican, Thai and Cajun, are likely options. In the north of the state, the living – and the cuisine – is more Southern, with Cajun-style options like shrimp gumbo and seafood jambalaya.

Pecan pie and the famous Key Lime Pie are popular desserts and widely available.

Captain Hornblower's Grill Room in Key West.

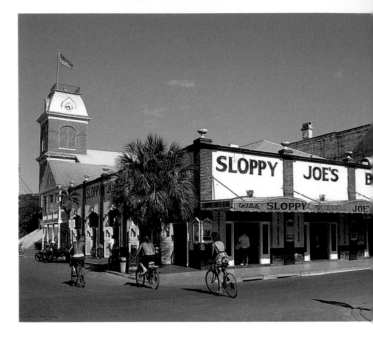

Be sure to sample a good Sunday brunch buffet, usually presented with pride as an edible art form. There may well be a dessert table, an omelette station with the chef awaiting your personal order, oysters shucked while you wait, a carving station with turkey, ham, tender beef or pork under poised knife, mushrooms in garlic, assorted cold cuts with dips – all displayed amid multicolored salads and fruits. Expect to pay around $20-25 for a spread like this, with a choice of drinks ranging from orange juice, coffee, iced tea, or hot herbal tea to a Champagne cocktail. Sunday brunch times vary, but are usually between 10am and 3pm.

Tips for Overseas Visitors

If meat or fish is described as grilled, it's cooked on a grill over an open flame. Otherwise, the term 'barbecue' relates to the sauce served with the meat, not the manner in which it is cooked.

While your dinner is being prepared you can order a bowl of something savory into which everyone in your party can dip – crab claws, perhaps, or hush puppies, deep-fried balls of cornmeal dough. Also, a salad course is traditionally served between starter and entrée (main course), and you may wish you had not ordered the latter.

Unless you enjoy batter, be sure to check with your server how your meal will be cooked. Delicately flavored grouper or soft-shell crab could well be smothered in batter and deep-fried, a preparation more common in northern Florida.

Alcoholic drinks are not necessarily available in eateries, though most places will serve beer and wine. Establishments offering fine dining will usually have a wine list.

Breakfasts are inexpensive and widely available from 7-11am in most areas. Fresh fruit, eggs cooked in a variety of ways, a stack of pancakes or French toast served with maple syrup, plenty of bacon slices, muffins, doughnuts, Danish pastries, juice, unlimited coffee ... all for a reasonable price.

The famed Sloppy Joe's Bar in Key West.

SHOPPING

Whether you want to buy a designer jacket, a 17C candle snuffer, or a pearl straight from the oyster, Florida provides the opportunity. Generally, the fashion scene in Florida is cool and casual, and each city and beach community has plenty of stores selling beachwear and smart casual clothes in its

shopping malls. These malls are served by
acres of parking space.

Two other interesting options await the
compulsive shopper: the flea market and the
outlet mall. This is a rare treat, particularly
for overseas visitors whose home countries
may have few such retailers. The flea market
at its best is a vast acreage of stalls selling
new and second-hand knick-knacks and
practical items.

Fort Lauderdale

The Swap Shop on West Sunrise Boulevard,
open from early morning to evening every
day of the year, provides more than 2,000
vendors selling new and used goods. It is an
indoor/outdoor entertainment center as well
as a flea market, and includes amusement
rides, a free circus, drive-in theater and a
video arcade. For upscale shopping in the

*Shopping at a
leisurely pace.*

city, try quaint **Las Olas Boulevard**, where horse-drawn carriages sweep by.

Sawgrass Mills, said to be one of the world's largest outlet malls, is 9 miles (14.5km) west of Fort Lauderdale at Sunrise Boulevard. It provides restaurants as well as stores selling straight-from-the-factory brand-name goods at up to 70 percent off normal retail prices.

Orlando

Claiming to be even bigger than Sawgrass Mills, is **Belz Factory Outlet World** at the north end of International Drive. They reckon 10 million people a year shop there. Almost every type of commodity is available in two massive enclosed malls and four shopping centers.

Visitors from outside the US should check that their electrical purchases will operate in their own country.

Flea World, open on Fridays, Saturdays and Sundays, is located between Orlando and Sanford (I-4, Exit 50 East to US 17-92, then right for 1 mile [1.5km]). It offers 1,600 stalls and live entertainment spread over more than 100 acres (40ha).

St Augustine

Here too there is an extensive **Outlet Center**, with more than 90 brand-name discount stores open daily. A free trolley shuttles shoppers around the complex.

Unusual gifts can be found in the specialty shops of St Augustine's **Historic District**, most of which is restricted to pedestrian traffic.

Jacksonville Area

The bright lights of Jacksonville (overleaf).

Historic **Avondale** in Jacksonville offers more than 60 boutiques, specialty shops,

galleries and restaurants, while **Jacksonville Landing**, right beside the St Johns River, features shops, eateries and entertainment.

For relentless seekers of antiques and collectibles, numerous towns and cities have pockets of stores catering to this demand, providing a compact happy hunting ground.

Shopping in a modern waterfront complex in Miami.

Beaches Antique Gallery, open all week and on Sunday afternoons at Jacksonville Beach, features more than 130 dealers offering a range of relics from the past.

Craft centers are useful places to find gifts and mementoes with a Florida flavor. The **Stephen Foster State Folk Culture Center** in White Springs offers a particularly good craft shop, much of the merchandise being created at the craft village on site.

Gainesville
Outside Gainesville, the streets of **Micanopy** are lined with antique shops.

Palm Beach
Worth Avenue, world-renowned for its landscaped blocks of upscale shopping, offers about 200 elegant boutiques and top-name shops, like Tiffany's and Saks Fifth Avenue, and expense-account restaurants.

Miami
There are internationally known stores in the Bal Harbor complex, while Greater Miami has a choice of shopping areas – Cocowalk in Coconut Grove, Lincoln Road Mall in South Beach and Bayside Marketplace in downtown Miami are among the famous areas.

ENTERTAINMENT AND NIGHTLIFE

Orlando
Entertainment is pretty well non-stop in Orlando. You'd think there's enough going on in the major theme parks to satisfy most tourists, but the list of things to do and watch seems endless. You can even see fireworks there every night of the year.

The city's leading entertainment center is **Church Street Station**, right in the heart of the historic downtown area. The former railroad depot and its associated warehouses and hotels have been turned into a complex of bars, discos, restaurants and shops.

The place is open daily from before lunch to after midnight, but it really swings into life after dark. That's when the collection of historic vehicles – including a 1932 Rolls-

In the heart of Orlando is Church Street Station, an entertainment and shopping complex.

Rosie O'Grady's Good Time Emporium provides entertainment while you drink (above right).

Royce and a Packard of 1933 – may be accompanied by a jazz band striking up on the sidewalk. Crowds gather and the tempo increases as more music – Dixieland Jazz, Rock & Roll classics, contemporary dance hits – pours from buildings on each side of the street. And what music! From **The Cheyenne Saloon and Opera House** – a vibrant piece of the Wild West – you'll hear Country & Western and Grand Old Opry-style too.

Rosie O'Grady's Good Time Emporium features red velvet, brass chandeliers and etched glass – each piece of furniture a genuine antique. You can hear Dixieland jazz and songs while watching chorus girls can-can on the bar.

Elsewhere on Church Street, you'll find folk and bluegrass, singing fudge-makers and roller-skating waitresses. At **Phineas Phogg's Balloon Works**, surrounded by decor honoring famous balloonists and their historic flights, you can dance the night away to high-energy recorded music.

If your idea of a good laugh is to be scared stiff, you need walk no farther than the corner of Orange Avenue to find **Terror on Church Street**, a combined theater and house of horrors which has a Dracula's Castle theme and the latest terrifying technology.

Pleasure Island, part of the Walt Disney World complex out at Lake Buena Vista, is where they hold that nightly New Year's Eve party – complete with fireworks. It's a 6-acre (2.4-ha) waterfront village of astonishing discos and strange nightclubs – places where bands play from a UFO and dancers rock and roll in a wind tunnel.

Themed dinner shows are another popular feature of the Orlando area's entertainment scene. Carefully stage-managed, the shows are usually presented twice nightly and it's fair to say that the food is less spectacular than the performances it accompanies.

Arabian Nights Dinner Attraction serves skillful horsemanship and flashing scimitars with a meal of prime rib. **Capone's Dinner and Show** has a Chicago speakeasy theme, with gangsters, molls, cops and Italian food.

Costumed wenches serve a 'banquet' of roast chicken and ribs and entertainment is provided by minstrels, magicians and jesters at **King Henry's Feast**. At **Medieval Times** diners eat chicken with their fingers amid bouts of jousting, sword play and mock-battles involving ball-and-chains, axes and other noisy weapons.

There's more mayhem at **Sleuth's Mystery Dinner Show**, where a murder mystery unfolds as diners enjoy their meal. **Wild Bill's Wild West Dinner Extravaganza** at

Kissimmee's Fort Liberty features Cowboys, Indians and the US Cavalry.

After all that, Orlando's nightclubs, mostly found in the major hotels, may seem rather conventional. They feature lots of piano bars, the newest of which – **Blazing Pianos**, in the Mercado Village on International Drive – is said to be the nation's only three-piano bar. The three fire-engine-red Yamaha grands are played simultaneously in a bar that seats 400.

You'd expect the major resort areas to offer a good range of entertainment and nightlife, but in many other parts of Florida these may merge in the tinkling notes of a piano in a hotel bar. Nevertheless, there are a number of surprises.

Miami

Coconut Grove, one of Miami's oldest 'village' neighborhoods, has a number of fashionable nightclubs. The **Coconut Grove Playhouse**, formerly a cinema, is the home of South Florida's leading professional theater company, renowned for performances of Broadway and off-Broadway shows. **Coral Gables** offers the Miracle Mile shopping area and famous restaurants.

Jazz musicians in Miami.

Other Areas

Greater Fort Lauderdale boasts a dozen
major theaters, including two in the massive
Broward Center for the Performing Arts,
and a number of others in neighboring
Hollywood and Pompano Beach.

Sarasota also has good arts facilities, with
two large performing arts centers and its own
philharmonic orchestra. Noted for its nightclubs, Sarasota's range from the downtown
Gator Club, which presents nightly live
bands, to **In Extremis**, a contemporary hot
spot with dancing to Top-40 tunes and a
spectacular laser, light and sound show.

Jacksonville's main entertainment center
is **Jacksonville Landing**, a $50 million com-
bined shopping mall and pier alongside the
St Johns River. Live shows are presented on
the central, open-air stage, but the nearby
clubs and bars also offer entertainment. The
city has a number of lively nightclubs.

Sedate Tallahassee, with its shady streets
and slow, Southern pace, casts its legislative
character aside when the sun goes down.
Bars spring into life all over town, and visitors
can catch live music at clubs and lounges like
Andrew's and **Po'Boys Creole Café**.

SPORTS AND ACTIVITIES

Outdoor leisure pursuits are a feature of life
in Florida, but there's no need to be an
expert to take part, nor to worry about
taking special equipment with you.
Instruction is available for all levels of
experience in many activities, and everything
from fishing equipment to sailboats and
horses can be rented. Local visitor
information centers can tell you what's
available and where you can rent equipment.

Paragliding in Fort Lauderdale.

On the Ground

Florida offers well over 1,100 golf courses –
more than in any other state in the Union.
Layouts range from Scottish-style links to flat
and hilly tracts. Many courses have been
designed by the world's top golfing names –
the likes of Nicklaus and Fazio. It's been
estimated that some 55 million rounds of golf
are played annually on the state's fairways,
and each year Florida plays host to about 20
professional golf tournaments. Top-class
instruction is available at the **Arnold Palmer
Golf Academy** in Orlando.

The state has more than 7,700 tennis
facilities, so enthusiasts won't have to travel
far to find somewhere suitable. Many of the
larger hotels have their own courts and
teaching facilities. The problem is not so
much finding an open court to play on, but
choosing a surface. You can play on clay,
grass, or hard courts.

Some resorts, like **The Westin Innisbrook
Resort** at Tarpon Springs, north of St
Petersburg on the west coast, are renowned
centers for both golf and tennis. The
Innisbrook features five championship golf
courses on which international tournaments
have been played, and 18 tennis courts.
Coaching is available from world-status
players.

Horseback riding is widely available, and
riding trails can be found in 16 state parks.
One of these is the **Paynes Prairie State
Preserve** at Micanopy, 10 miles (16km) south
of Gainesville. This 20,000-acre (8,094-ha)
preserve was one of Florida's first cattle
grazing areas, used by both Indians and early
settlers. In 1774, the artist and naturalist
William Bartram described it as 'the great
Alachua savannah'.

On the Water

Watersports are a way of life on the coast and along the state's many rivers, lakes, springs and inland waterways. The best surfing is to be found off the beaches of the Atlantic coast, especially between Daytona Beach and the Jacksonville Beaches, but there are also good locations in the Panhandle. Waterskiing and jetskiing are practiced all along the coast, but there are restrictions on fast-moving vessels of any kind on many inland waterways and rivers because of erosion and the threat to wildlife.

Canoes and kayaks are the best craft to use for exploring the real Florida. For a taste of adventure without isolation – in a guided group tour, perhaps – go to a company like Adventures Unlimited at Milton, just north of Pensacola, where several rivers in the **Blackwater State Forest** can be traversed by canoe, kayak, or raft.

With so many miles of coastline, sailing is a popular sport in the Sunshine State. This yacht is gliding past St Petersburg's pier.

Tubing (riding on a tire inner tube on slow-moving rivers or in springs), hiking, biking and camping are available. The company will provide home-cooking for groups of 15 or more.

Other popular places for canoe explorations are the Suwannee River in the northwest, the Myakka River near Sarasota, the Ten Thousand Islands area at the southwest edge of the Everglades and in the Keys. Again, some of the best canoeing locations are to be found in the state parks – 46 feature canoe trails and most of those offer canoe rentals.

Sport fishing is a favorite pursuit, and anglers can be seen fishing almost anywhere – bridges, piers, beaches, from boats off-shore and on rivers and lakes. Fishermen will need to obtain a license from a tackle shop, where they may also rent gear.

Canoeing is one of the best ways to discover 'real' Florida.

Deep-sea game-fishing excursions – for trophies like marlin, pompano, sailfish and shark, and for table fish like red snapper and grouper – are offered at marinas around the coast. The most favored places are Daytona Beach, Islamorada, Key West, St John's Pass Village at Madeira Beach, near St Petersburg, Panama City – and Boca Grande for tarpon fishing off its shores.

You can snorkel and scuba-dive in the clear waters off the southeast coast and around the Keys, and explore the many wrecks that lie offshore, including ancient Spanish treasure ships. If you think the treasure tales are far-fetched, stop at Mel Fisher's **Maritime Heritage Museum** on Key West to see the fortune in recovered gold and silver on display there.

In the Air

Central Florida is a great place for hot-air ballooning, and it's not unusual on mornings or evenings when the wind is light to see a dozen or more colorful balloons floating above Orlando. About half a dozen companies offer flights to visitors, and the fee – around $100 – includes round-trip transit from your hotel, plus champagne.

At Clermont in Lake County, less than an hour's drive north of Orlando, you can take a flight in a glider, or take lessons if you like. The place to head for is **Seminole Lake Gliderport**.

If you want to know what it's like to take part in a World-War-II-style dog fight, **Fighter Pilots USA** at Kissimmee, south of Orlando, will not only show you – they will let you find out for yourself by actually flying a plane with guidance from a pilot instructor.

THE BASICS

This guide is for both overseas visitors as well as people from the US and Canada. Some details therefore will not apply to everyone. Sections of particular reference to non-US residents are marked with an asterisk [*].

Before You Go *

Citizens of the 21 countries participating in the Visa Waiver Pilot Program (VWPP) – including those from the UK and New Zealand – no longer need a visa to enter the US for a period of up to 90 days. All that is required is a valid passport, and a visa waiver form, which may be obtained in advance from a travel agent or provided by the airline during check-in. This form must be handed in to immigration on arrival. For a list of countries participating in the scheme, contact your nearest American Embassy. Vaccinations are not required.

Getting There *

Direct flights arrive at Miami and Orlando from all over the world, although from some places a transfer will have to be made at another airport in the US. Fares vary widely according to season, and it is worth remembering that November to April is the peak tourist season

south of Orlando, while May to October is a more popular time for visiting the northern part of the state. Inevitably these times will be the most expensive at which to travel, and you are advised to shop around to get the best deal on flights.

Low-cost flights can be arranged through flight agents or by booking a charter flight, and APEX or Super-APEX tickets may be bought directly from the airlines. The travel ads in the Sunday papers or the various listing magazines are the best places to look.

Fly-drive and flight-plus-accommodation deals can work out cheaper than booking everything separately, and brochures on these types of vacations are available from travel agents.

Arriving *

An immigration form and a customs declaration must be completed during the flight, and handed in once you land. You will be asked where you plan to spend the first night, and when you intend to leave the country. You might also be asked to prove that you can support yourself financially during your stay, and any indication that you cannot might result in admission being refused. To expedite your progress through customs, pay special attention to Question 9 on your declaration form; this relates to fruit, plants, meats, food, soil, live animals (including birds) and farm products.

Orlando International Airport is 9 miles (14km) from downtown Orlando, and is well served by shuttle buses, local buses and taxis. Miami International Airport, 6 miles (10km) from the city, is similarly served, and both the Greyhound terminal and train station are within easy reach. Some hotels provide transfers from the airport, and car rental companies shuttle passengers to their lots. There are also international airports at Tampa, West Palm Beach, Daytona Beach, Jacksonville, St Petersburg/Clearwater, Fort Lauderdale and Key West (but without jet service).

The Greyhound bus is a cheap way to get around

Accidents and Breakdowns

Check to see if your initial car rental charge includes CDW (collision damage waiver), a form of insurance that covers the car you are driving. It is not cheap at between $9 and $13 a day, but without it you are liable for every scratch and bump on the car. If it does not come as part of the deal it is well worth adding it on, unless your own policy covers you.

An emergency number will be given to you to call, in case your rental car breaks down. Otherwise raise your car hood and wait for the highway patrol or state police to come by. A mobile phone (a lifeline in an emergency) can be rented from the rental car agency.

Accommodations

Staying in Florida can be surprisingly cheap, and there is a wide variety of accommodations to choose from. Motel rooms are usually of a reasonable size, with some double bedrooms easily sleeping up to four people –

families will benefit from the system in many motels that charges by the room, not the number of people.

Those traveling on their own fare worst, with single rooms being doubles rented at a slightly reduced rate. There is a difference between hotels and motels. Large hotels and upscale beach resorts prefer you to make a reservation. Motels are generally located beside main roads away from city centers; most rooms come with bathroom, TV, and phone.

Large or budget hotels do not include breakfast in the price, although B&Bs or special package deals usually will. Bed and breakfast in private houses is now on the increase, and though not necessarily the cheap option it can be in Europe, it offers a chance to stay in a homey atmosphere with the prospect of a satisfying breakfast to start the day.

Accommodations equipped with kitchens in low- and moderately-priced hotels, or in condominiums, are also

popular.

Backpackers and low-budget travelers will not find the wide choice of accommodations in the US that they do in other countries, but the situation is improving and more hostels are being provided, like the Miami Beach International Hostel, 1438 Washington Avenue, Miami Beach, FL 33139; ☎ 305/534-2988. A useful publication is *The Hostelling International Guide for Africa, America, Asia and the Pacific*, which includes details of youth hostels in Florida.

The Don Cesar Hotel on the seafront at St Petersburg.

Hotel and motel chains (Toll-free/freephone within the US):
Best Western: ☎ 800/528-1234.
Comfort Inn: ☎ 800/228-5150.
Hilton: ☎ 800/445-8667.
Holiday Inn: ☎ 800/465-4329.
Marriott Hotels & Resorts:
☎ 800/228-9290.
Quality Inns: ☎ 800/228-5151.
Ramada Inn: ☎ 800/272-6232.
Sheraton Hotels: ☎ 800/325-3535.
Westin Hotels & Resorts:
☎ 800/228-3000.

The Centennial Fountain bursts through the gathering dusk at Orlando.

Airports see Arriving p.108

Banks
These are open on weekdays as follows:
Monday to Thursday 9am-3pm; Friday 9am-5pm, although longer opening hours are becoming more normal. Most banks change foreign travelers' checks (cheques) and currency, though it may be cheaper to conduct these transactions at exchange services as they charge less commission.

With Mastercard or Visa you may withdraw cash at any bank which displays the relevant signs, and holders of Diners

The crystal-clear waters at Key Biscayne are a beach-lover's dream.

and American Express cards can obtain cash at specified outlets – check before you leave home.

Bicycles
Bikes can be rented quite cheaply by the day or the week, and outlets are usually plentiful near beaches, university campuses and in places that are particularly good for cycling. Many big cities have bike lanes. For a small fee, Greyhound buses will carry bikes provided they are boxed,

and Amtrak charges a few dollars for putting a bike on board.

The problem with cycling in Florida is the traffic, the huge trucks and camper vans being particularly unpleasant, and the interstate must be avoided. Check with the tourist office for details of organized cycle tours, reputable bike shops and advice on bike paths and long-distance cycling.

Breakdowns *see* **Accidents**

Buses *see* **Transportation**

Camping

Camping in Florida is provided on a very grand scale, and includes a mixture of huge national and state parks as well as privately-run camping sites. Hikers or campers seeking the minimum of fuss will favor campsites in the rural backwoods with few facilities to jar the peace and harmony of their surroundings. Those traveling in recreational vehicles (RVs) might prefer the more elaborate sites that cater to every camping need, and often include laundry facilities and a grocery shop.

On-site trailer and tent rental is offered by many site owners, but booking in advance is recommended, especially during the winter months. Increasingly popular is hiring an RV from a company that allows you to start and end at different places, with airport transfers thrown in. (Note that it is often cheaper to do this in advance before you travel, if you live outside the US.)

Car Rental *

Rental cars are widely available through airports, hotels or individual companies, and car rental is cheaper in Florida than anywhere else in the US. The minimum rental age is 21, although some companies impose a limit of 25, and others increase insurance premiums for those under 25. You will be expected to pay by credit card, otherwise a large deposit may be demanded.

Arranging fly/drive or booking a car before arriving in Florida can be extremely economical. Try to get free unlimited mileage, and check in advance if there will be a drop-off charge for leaving the car somewhere other than where you hired it. Scrutinize the small print of your rental agreement for mention of collision damage waiver (CDW), and if this is not included in the price, do seriously consider buying it (*see* **Accidents and Breakdowns**).

Car rental companies: (toll-free/freephone within the US)
Alamo: ☎ 800/327-9633.
Avis: ☎ 800/331-1212.
Budget: ☎ 800/527-0700.
Hertz: ☎ 800/654-3131.
National: ☎ 800/227-7368.
Thrifty: ☎ 800/331-4200.

Children

Florida is extremely child-friendly, and with its easy lifestyle and holiday atmosphere, it is especially welcoming towards families. Children under 18 can often stay free in their parents' room in many hotels. Restaurants, particularly the national chains, frequently offer special menus, small portions and games.

Many tourist attractions and museums offer reduced rates for younger visitors, and facilities for baby-changing may be available in larger sights. Although there are discounts for travel of all kinds, perhaps the most comfortable way to survive long journeys with kids is by train or car. Beware of the hot Florida sun, and cover up children's delicate skin even when lining up for rides or sightseeing. Hats are essential, and sun-block should always be worn.

Churches *see* **Religion**

Climate *see* p.82

Clothing

Informality is the keynote in Florida, and it is best to wear casual and comfortable clothing, especially when traveling. A very few restaurants and hotels expect more formal attire, but shops and eating places off the beach usually require that you cover up and don footwear.

Remember that evenings can be considerably cooler than the daytime. Air-conditioning makes theaters, restaurants and shops quite chilly, so an extra sweater or jacket can be essential. *See also* **Etiquette**.

* Measurements are still imperial, as the US has yet to go metric. Clothing sizes are always two figures less than they are in the UK, with the exception of men's suits and shirts which are identical.

Dress Sizes

UK	8	10	12	14	16	18
US	6	8	10	12	14	16

Women's Shoes

UK	4.5	5	5.5	6	6.5	7
US	6	6.5	7	7.5	8	8.5

Men's Shoes

UK	7	7.5	8.5	9.5	10.5	11
US	8	8.5	9.5	10.5	11.5	12

Complaints

Complaints about goods or services should be made at the time, if possible. At a hotel or restaurant, make your complaint calmly to the manager. For more serious complaints, contact the police or the tourist office (*see* **Tourist Information Offices**).

Consulates *

Embassies and consulates can be found at the following addresses:

British Consulate:
1001 Brickell Bay Drive, Ste 2110
Miami, Florida 33131;
☎ 305/374-1522.

Australian Embassy:
1601 Massachusetts Avenue NW,
Washington DC 20036-2273;
☎ 202/797-3000.

Canadian Embassy:
200 S Biscayne Boulevard,
Suite 1600, Miami FL 33131
☎ 305/579-1600.

Irish Embassy:
2234 Massachusetts Avenue NW,
Washington DC 20008;
☎ 202/462-3939.

New Zealand Embassy:
37 Observatory Circle NW,
Washington DC 20008;
☎ 202/328-4800.

Crime

Crime in Florida has been well publicized recently, but apart from a few trouble spots like the Overtown and Liberty City districts of Miami, the state is in fact a relatively safe place. As in many major cities, mugging is a constant problem, and a few precautions are recommended to reduce the likelihood of becoming a victim:

- try not to look too obviously like a tourist
- don't flash money around
- stick to busy tourist areas, especially at night-time; find out where the dangerous areas are, and avoid them
- if confronted by a mugger, the best thing is to hand over whatever is being demanded; keep a small wad of notes handy as a precaution – if the worst happens this might be sufficient to satisfy the mugger
- keep valuables locked in your hotel safe
- never open your room door to anyone unless you know who it is (i.e. room service, housekeeping)
- if someone rear-ends your car, don't stop. Head to nearest police station or commercial area.

If your passport is stolen, report this immediately to the nearest Consulate. Keep travelers' checks (cheques) separate from the list of their numbers, and in the event of theft, report the loss using the telephone number supplied by the issuer.

Car crimes against tourists in Florida have also been well reported, and rental cars in Florida should now have nothing to identify them as such. Advice to drivers includes ignoring anyone trying to flag you down, and not stopping if someone rams you 'accidentally' from behind. Common sense would warn against stopping in seedy urban areas, even in the day time. Keep doors locked and windows wound fully up when driving through busy areas. When parking the car, always lock valuables out of sight.

Currency see **Money**

Customs and Entry Regulations see **Arriving** p.108

Disabled Visitors
By the standards of most other countries, the US provides exceptional facilities for the disabled, thanks to the 1990 Americans with Disabilities Act.

Much public transport is equipped to take wheelchairs, and attendants traveling with disabled people can often travel free.

All public buildings must by law be wheelchair accessible and provide suitable toilet facilities, and most street corners have sloping curbs. There are also lower public telephones, special stalls in public lavatories, Braille indicators in elevators and an increasing number of reserved parking places. Attractions generally accept disabled visitors, and efforts are made to ease their way and provide necessary comforts.

Tourist offices have relevant information for disabled travelers (see **Tourist Information Offices**), and local telephone directories list support groups for the disabled. Larger hotels have specially designed rooms which should be booked in advance. Major rental car firms (see **Car Rental**) provide cars with hand controls at no extra cost, although these are limited and early booking is advised. For further information, consult the *Planning Guide for Travelers with Disabilities* ☎ 888/735-2872 (toll-free/freephone within the US).

All roads are well signposted.

Driving *

In Florida driving is on the right-hand side. Foreign nationals may drive in the US on a full driving license, and fuel is cheap (some self-service stations may require you to pay before they release the pump). Speed limits are as follows: 25mph (40kph) in school zones, 35mph (56kph) within city limits, 50-55mph (72-88kph) on major highways and 65mph (105kph) on interstates. Be aware of the posted speed limits at all times.

You should also note that slower traffic tends to keep to the right-hand lane.

Florida's Turnpike, and certain major expressways, are toll roads. In Florida you may turn right on a red light – after stopping – unless otherwise indicated. Parking can be a problem, and illegally parked vehicles are towed away or given a ticket. Look for a parking lot, or designated meter parking.

Remember that everyone in the car must wear a seat belt. *See also* **Car Rental** and **Accidents and Breakdowns**.

Electric Current *

All personal appliances run on 110 volts AC, and most sockets are designed to take flat two-pronged plugs. Visitors will need an adaptor for their appliances, which may be bought from electrical goods stores or borrowed from the front desk of large hotels. Those appliances rated for other voltages will need a transformer.

Embassies *see* Consulates

Emergencies

Simply dial 911 in an emergency, and the appropriate emergency service will be summoned quickly. Try to give accurate directions, including hotel name, street name and nearest cross-section if you can.

Call boxes have been installed on interstate highways at 1 mile (1.6km) intervals, and from one of these you can call for help without dialing 911.

In cases of dire distress your Consulate might help, but this will be limited. *See also* **Health**.

Etiquette *

Floridians are particularly laid-back, and do not easily take offence. Topless sunbathing for women, however, is not only frowned on but is actually illegal. Women accustomed to being topless on the beach in Europe will be in for a shock if they try it here.

For dress code, *see* under **Clothing** (above).

Excursions

Cruise to the Bahamas, the Caribbean, Mexico and South America from the Port of Miami (biggest cruise port in the world with 3 million passengers annually), Port Everglades in Fort Lauderdale and Tampa. There are many organized tours inland too, especially of the Everglades. *See* **Tourist Information Offices**.

For a different way to see Florida, try a cruise on the Jungle Queen *at Fort Lauderdale.*

Guidebooks *see* **Maps**

Health *

For tourists from outside the US travel insurance is essential, as there is no national health system to provide medical coverage, and private health care is extremely expensive. Travel agents and tour companies will recommend a suitable policy, and the coverage should include at least $1,000,000 for medical expenses.

If you have a serious accident during your stay, you will be cared for first and asked to pay later. For non-emergencies, look under Physicians and Surgeons or Clinics in the Yellow Pages, but remember to keep all receipts and documentation so that you can claim back any money you spend. Larger towns have walk-in medical and dental clinics listed in the telephone directory. For minor problems the drugstore offers a huge selection of remedies.

If you know in advance that you will need drugs while you are in the US, get your doctor to make out a generic prescription of your medication (without name brands).

A common problem when vacationing in Florida is sunburn, and visitors are advised to cover up, drink plenty of water and only gradually attempt to get a tan.

Hours *see* **Opening Hours**

Information *see* **Tourist Information Offices**

Language *

Although Spanish is the second language in parts of Florida, especially the south, and widely spoken by its many Hispanic inhabitants, English is still the main language.

American English	British English
Restroom	Public toilet
Bathroom	Private toilet
Chips	Crisps
Broiled	Grilled
No standing	No parking or stopping
Do not pass	No overtaking
Sidewalk	Pavement
Pavement	Roadway
1st floor	Ground floor
2nd floor	1st floor, etc.
Line	Queue
Subway	Underground
Drugstore	Chemist
Trailer	Caravan
Pants	Trousers
To go	Take-away (food)
Shrimp	King prawn
Check	Bill

Watch out, however, for some confusion with American terms which can be quite different from the English version! A few of the most confusing are shown in the panel.

Laundry
Many larger hotels offer laundry and dry-cleaning services, and there are coin-operated laundromats and launderettes as well as dry-cleaning establishments throughout Florida.

Lost Property
Report any lost items as soon as you realize they are missing. In hotels, check with the front desk or hotel security. Local telephone directories list the numbers of cab companies and public transport, and the police should be informed of any lost travel documents.

Try to obtain a police report if you intend filing claims for valuable items. Lost or stolen credit cards and travelers' checks (cheques) should be reported immediately to the issuing company with a list of numbers, and the police should also be informed.

Maps
Free maps and brochures, provided by State Tourist Offices, visitor centers and Chambers of Commerce are fine for general route planning and driving. A large-scale motoring map is ideal for serious touring, and may be obtained from any bookshop and most gas stations. State and national parks issue maps of scenic drives, hikes and trails when you enter the parks. The *Michelin Green Guide Florida* contains detailed maps and information on the main sights and attractions in Florida. *See* Tourist Information Offices.

Medical Care see Health

Money *
Dollar bills are all the same size and color – green – so check the different denominations carefully: they come in $1, $5, $10, $20, $50 and $100s. Coins are half a dollar (50 cents), a quarter (25 cents), a dime (10 cents), a nickel (5 cents) and a penny (one cent).

Instead of bringing cash, carry large amounts in dollar travelers' checks (cheques) which are widely accepted, or use a credit card. There is a state tax of 6% throughout Florida on everything you buy (except store-bought food) but is not part of the marked price. There may also be varied local taxes (e.g. on lodging). *See also* **Banks**.

Newspapers

The national daily *USA Today* is on sale in self-service news bins in every Florida town, and the *New York Times* and the *Wall Street Journal* can be bought at newsstands. Foreign newspapers may be found in busy tourist areas. Otherwise the main Florida cities all have their own daily newspapers, such as the *Miami Herald*, and most communities produce weekly bulletins.

Opening Hours

Drugstores: 9am-9pm daily, with some open 24 hours. Offices: 8 or 9am-5 or 6pm, Monday to Friday.
Shops:
Supermarkets: 8am-9pm, Monday to Saturday; 8am-7pm, Sunday. Some open 24 hours. Downtown: 10am-6pm, Monday to Friday; 10am-1pm or 6pm, Saturday. Malls: 10am-9pm, Monday to Saturday; 10am-6pm, Sunday.
Banks: 9am-3pm, Monday to Thursday; 9am-5pm, Friday. Some banks are now staying open for longer periods. *See also* **Post Offices.**

Photography

Film is readily available from camera shops, but is usually less expensive at drugstores and supermarkets.

Police *

American police are generally helpful and obliging when things go wrong for foreign travelers. In an emergency you can get a quick response by dialing 911. There are three types of police in the US: the City Force, the Sheriff, whose domain is outside the city limits, and the Highway Patrol, who deal with traffic accidents and offenses beyond the city limits.

Post Offices

Local post offices are generally open from 9am-4:30 or 5pm, though these times may vary. Stamps may also be bought from machines at the post office or in business districts, or from hotels and drugstores. Blue mail boxes are located on the sidewalk.

Ordinary mail within the US costs 32c for a letter weighing up to one ounce (28g), and letters must include the zip code. Air mail between the US and Europe takes about a week; postcards cost 40c, aerograms are 50c, and letters weighing up to half an ounce (14g) are 60c. There are strict rules about sending parcels, which must be contained in special packaging sold by the post office and sealed according to instructions.

Public Holidays

New Year's Day: 1 January
Martin Luther King Jr's
Birthday: 15 January
President's Day: 3rd Monday in
February
Easter Monday
Memorial Day: Last Monday in
May
Independence Day: 4 July; the
biggest national holiday
Labor Day: 1st Monday in
September
Columbus Day: 2nd Monday in
October
Veterans' Day: 11 November
Thanksgiving Day: last
Thursday in November
Christmas Day: 25 December
On these days, all federal and
state government offices are
closed. Shops, banks and
offices are likely to be closed
all day. In some places Good
Friday is a half-day holiday.

Public Transport see
Transportation

Religion

America is a melting pot of all
the nationalities of the world,
and just about every religious
group is represented here.
Catholic churches are easy to
find in Miami, thanks to its
Hispanic population, and most
communities are served by
churches of several denominations. For information on the
different services available,
contact the local Chamber of
Commerce or look in the
Yellow Pages.

Smoking *

Smoking is frowned on in the
US, though not as severely in
Florida as in health-conscious
California. Many restaurants
provide separate areas for
smoking, although it is banned
in cinemas, elevators, public
transport and many public
buildings.

Stamps see Post Offices

Taxis see Transportation

Telephones *

Half a dozen companies run
the Florida telephone system.
Only two of these will route
overseas calls: AT&T and ITT.
The easiest way to make an
overseas call is from a hotel
room, and although this costs
more, it can save a lot of time
and energy. Or dial 0 for the
Operator and call collect
(overseas credit cards are also
valid).

To dial direct from a public
phone, dial 011 plus country
code (44 for the UK, 353 for
Ireland, 61 for Australia, 64 for
New Zealand) plus area code
plus telephone number, and
make sure you have plenty of

For a break from the highways, take a trip in a yellow water taxi from the seafront in Miami.

money in small coins. The lowest rate for international calls to Europe is generally between 6pm and 7am, and the same is true for non-local and long-distance calls with the US.

There are well over 100 area codes in the US, and nine in Florida: northwest (Tallahassee) – 850; northeast (Jacksonville) – 904; mid-west (Gainesville) – 352; west central (Tampa) – 813; southwest Ft Myers) – 941; east central (Orlando) – 407; central southeast (West Palm Beach) – 561; southeast (Ft Lauderdale) – 954; extreme south (Miami) – 305. To call within the area code, dial 1 plus telephone number; to dial outside the area code, dial 1 plus area code plus number. All 800 numbers (toll-free/freephone within the US) must be prefixed with 1.

Time Difference

Florida operates under two time zones: while Eastern Standard Time (Greenwich Mean Time minus 5 hours) covers most of the state, the Panhandle region west of the Apalachicola River observes Central Standard Time (GMT minus 6 hrs). All clocks are set forward one hour for Daylight Saving from the first Sunday in April until the last in October.

Tipping *

The accepted – and expected – rates are 15 percent in restaurants and for taxis, 10–20 percent for hairdressers and barbers, and 10 percent for bartenders and cocktail servers.

Chambermaids should receive $2 after a few day's stay, porters about $1 per bag, and doormen $1 for hailing a cab.

Toilets *

Known as restrooms or powder rooms in the US, toilets are found in all restaurants, large stores and hotels. Usually they are free, but if not you will need a dime. If there is an attendant, remember to leave a tip.

Tourist Information Offices

Tourists are well catered to in Florida. Most towns have a Chamber of Commerce useful for information, maps, etc. and each area also has a Tourist Office. The Florida Tourism Industry Marketing Corporation (FTIMC) is at 661 E Jefferson Street, Suite 300, Tallahassee, Florida 32302 ☎ 904/488 5607. Contact them via the American Embassy in your own country, and ask them for a list of tourist information offices in specific parts of Florida. The FTIMC has offices at: Roebuck

House, First Floor, Palace Street, London SW1E 5BA; ☎ 1716 306602, and at 121 Bloor Street East, Suite 1003, Toronto, Ontario M4W 3M5, Canada.

State-run Welcome Centers are found along the highway close to state borders, and they offer tourist information and coupons for cut-rate accommodations and food. Convention and Visitors Bureaus, or visitor centers, also carry plenty of information on local areas, and there are free newspapers that list entertainments in most communities.

Transportation

Driving is the best way to get around Florida, and the roads are well maintained. *See also* **Car Rental**.

For those traveling on a low budget or keen to see the country with the minimum of effort, the Greyhound bus connects nearly 150 Florida destinations. It is possible to pick up local bus services to reach the places in between, although in very rural areas these services are infrequent.

Florida is also quite well served by Amtrak rail service, which connects over 20 major cities in the state.

Air travel is cheaper than in Europe, provided that you book in advance. There are at least nine major airports dotted around key parts of Florida.

Taxi cabs can be picked up at hotels, airports, and bus and rail stations. Check out the trams or water taxis that serve some of the more populated water fronts of Florida.

TV and Radio

Most hotels and motels subscribe to cable TV with around 30 television channels to choose from. It is possible to watch for free round-the-clock news, sport, films and music (with frequent commercial breaks), but you will be charged for watching movies on premium channels.

Many big games are shown on network channels free of charge. Major sporting events, however, are transmitted on a pay-as-you-view basis – $40 for a world heavyweight boxing match is not uncommon.

Radio stations are even more numerous, though in some rural areas only one or two may be received.

Vaccinations *see* Before You Go p.108

Youth Hostels *see* Accommodations

INDEX

Amelia Island 70
Apalachicola 68
Apalachicola National Forest 68
Arcadia
  All-Florida Championship Rodeo 84
Asolo Center for the Performing Arts 55
Asolo Theater 55
Astronaut Hall of Fame 79
Atlantic Coast 75-81
Atlantis 80

Big Cypress National Preserve 45
Big Lagoon 63
Boyd Hill Nature Park 56
British Colonists 14
Broward Center for the Performing Arts 102

Canaveral National Seashore 79
  North Beach 79
Cape Canaveral 79
Captiva Island 12, 50
Carabelle 68
Caryville International Worm Fiddling Contest 86
Cassadaga 35
Cedar Key 61
  Dock Street 61
Central Florida 28-35
Charles Hosmer Morse Gallery of Art 34
Chinese Showcase 29
Clearwater Beach 58, 60
Cocoa Beach 74
Coral Castle 40
Crackers 23
Cubans 22
Cypress Gardens 27, 34

Davie 81
Daytona Beach 76
Daytona Beach Motorcycle Week 84
DeLand 35
  Cracker Day 84
Dry Tortugas National Park 45

Edison's Home 53
Emerald Coast 64
entertainment and nightlife 97-102
Everglades 8-10, 48-49

Flamingo Visitor Center 49
Ten Thousand Islands 49

Fernandina Beach 70
  Shrimp Festival 84
Flagler, Henry Morrison 17, 45, 80
Flamingo Gardens and Arboretum 81
Flatlands 8
Florida Aquarium 27
Florida Caverns State Park 66
Florida Keys 40
Florida National Trail 46
food and drink 88-91
Fort Clinch State Park 70
Fort Lauderdale 77
  Las Olas Boulevard 93
  Sawgrass Mills 93
  Swap Shop 92
Fort Myers 53
Fort Pickens 62
Fort Walton Beach 64
  Gulfarium 64
  US Air Force Armament Museum 64
Fruit and Spice Park 40

Gainesville 71, 97
  The Devil's Milhopper State Geological Site 71
  Florida Museum of Natural History 71
  Harn Museum of Art 71
  Morningside Nature Center 71
Gatorland 33
Great Explorations 56
Greater Fort Lauderdale Film Festival 87
Gulf Coast 50-61
Gulf Islands National Seashore 62
Gulf World 64

Homosassa Springs State Park 60, 61
Homestead 40

J N 'Ding' Darling National Wildlife Refuge 52
Jacksonville 69, 93
  Anheuser-Busch Brewery 69
  Avondale 93
  Beaches Antique Gallery 97
  Cummer Gallery of Art and Gardens 69
  Jacksonville Landing 69, 96, 102
  Jazz Festival 87

Kingley Plantation 69
Museum of Science and History 69
Riverwalk 69
Stephen Foster State Folk Culture Center 97
Zoological Gardens 69
Jacksonville and the Beaches 69
John Pennekamp Coral Reef State Park 41
Jungle Queen 80

Kennedy Space Center 19, 27, 77, 78
  Rocket Garden 78
Key Largo 41
Key West 11, 43-44
  Aquarium 45
  Audubon House 45
  Conch Train 45
  Fantasy Fest 87
  Hemingway's House 45
  Sloppy Joe's Bar 45, 91
  Wreckers' Museum 45

Labelle Swamp Cabbage Festival 84
Lake Buena Vista 27
  Candlelight Processional 87
Lion Country Safari 27, 80

Marathon 42
  Museums of Crane Point Hammock 43
Marco Island 46
Marianna 66
Miami 37-40, 97, 101
  Coconut Grove 37, 101
  Coral Gables 37, 38, 101
  Gusman Center 39
  Little Havana 37
  Metro-Dade Cultural Center 39
  Metrozoo 37, 38
  Miami Art Museum 39
  Miami Seaquarium 39
  Miccosukee Arts Festival 87
  Museum of Science and Space Transit Planetarium 39
  Old Town Trolley Tour 37
  Vizcaya 39
Miami Beach 39
  Art Deco District 39
  Bass Museum of Art 40
Micanopy 97
Miracle Strip Amusement Park 64
Monkey Jungle 40

INDEX

Monticello Jefferson County
  Watermelon Festival 85
Mosquito Lagoon 79
Mount Dora 34

Naples 45
  Frannie's Teddy Bear
    Museum 46
National Historic Districts 35
North Fort Myers 53

Ocala 35
  Museum of Drag Racing 35
Ocala National Forest 35
Okeechobee 10
Old Cape Florida Lighthouse
  44
Orlando 28-35, 93, 97-101
  Belz Factory Outlet World 93
  Church Street Station 98
  Flea World 93
  Terror on Church Street 100
  Walt Disney World see Walt
    Disney World
Overseas Highway 17

Palm Beach 80, 97
  Henry M Flagler Museum 80
  Norton Museum of Art 80
Panama City Beach 64, 65
  Museum of Man in the Sea
    65
Panhandle 62-68
Parrot Jungle 40
Pensacola 62
  Great Gulfcoast Arts Festival
    87
  Gulf Breeze Zoo and
    Botanical Gardens 62
  Museums:
    Civil War Soldiers 62
    Museum of Art 62
    National Museum of Naval
      Aviation 62
    Pensacola Historical
      Museum 62
  Seafood Festival 86
  Wall South and Veterans'
    Memorial Park 62
Pensacola Beach 64
Pensacola Village 62
Perdido Key 63
Plant, Henry B 17
Playalinda Beach 79

Rivership Romance 35

Sanibel Island 50
Santa Rosa Island 63
Sarasota 53

Avenue of Flowers 54
Cà d'Zan 55
Museum of the Circus 55
Ringling Museum of Art 55
Sea World of Florida 27, 31
Seaside 64
Seminole Indians 15, 21-23
Shell Factory 53
Shell Island 65
Shipwreck Island Water Park
  64
shopping 91-97
Silver Springs 35
Space Coast 77
Spaceport USA 77
Spanish Explorers 13
Splendid China 31
sports and activities 102-107
St Andrew's State Recreation
  Area 65
St Augustine 15, 71, 73
  Alligator Farm 74
  Castillo de San Marcos 22, 72
  Colonial Historic District 73,
    93
  Flagler College 73
  Government House 74
  Lightner Museum 73
  Mission de Nombre de Dios
    74
  Oldest House 73
  Oldest Store Museum 73
  Oldest Wooden Schoolhouse
    73
  Outlet Center 93
  Spanish Night Watch 85
  Spanish Quarter 73

St Petersburg 55
  Colonial Gardens Hotel 56
  Florida Suncoast Dome 55
  Museum of Fine Arts 56
  Salvador Dali Museum 56
  Pier 55
Suwannee river 8,9

Tallahassee 16, 66, 102
  Calhoun Street 67
  Maclay State Gardens 68
  Museum of Florida History
    68
  Museum of History and
    Natural Science 67, 68
  New Capitol 67
  Old Capitol 67
  Old Town Trolley Tour 67
  Park Avenue 67
  Springtime Festival 84
Tampa 55-57
  Busch Gardens: The Dark

Continent 57, 59
Gasparilla Pirate Festival 84
Museums:
  Tampa Museum of Art 57
  Henry Plant Museum 57
  Museum of African-
    American Art 57
  Museum of Science and
    Industry 57
Tampa Bay's Performing
  Arts Center 57
Tampa Bay Hotel 57
Tarpon Springs 58
  Festival of Epiphany 83
  Spongeorama Exhibit Center
    58
Theatre of the Sea 42
Titusville 79

Universal Studios Florida 4,
  27, 30
  Animal Actors Show 31
  Back to the Future – the
    Ride 31
  Ghostbusters 31
  Hercules and Zena Show 31
  Psycho house 31
  Twister 31

Van Wezel Performing Arts
  Hall 55

Wakulla Springs 68
Walt Disney World 27-31
  Animal Kingdom 30
  Disney MGM Studios 27, 29
    Tower of Terror 30
  Epcot Center 26, 27, 29
    Future World 29
    Spaceship Earth 29
  Magic Kingdom 27, 28
    Adventureland 28
    Fantasyland 5, 28
    Frontierland 28
    Liberty Square 28
    Main Street USA 28
    Mickey's Starland 29
    Tomorrowland 28
  Pleasure Island 100
  Waterparks 30
Water Mania 32
weather 82-83
Wet 'n Wild 27, 32
White Springs Florida Folk
  Festival 84
Woodville 68
  Natural Bridge Battlefield
    State Historic Site 68

Ybor City Fiesta Day 84